FLAWED BEAUTY

"BEAUTY THAT IS IMPERFECT, IMPERMANENT AND INCOMPLETE."

NITYA KISHORE

Contents

1. Imperfection Is Perfection — 1

2. Chapter 2 — 3

3. Beauty Of Flaws — 4

4. Chapter 4 — 6

5. Beauty Lies In The Eyes Of The Beholder — 7

6. The Beauty Of Perspectives. — 9

7. Chapter 7 — 11

8. Paradox Of A Mirror — 15

9. The Silent Wisdom Of A Candle — 17

10. A Feather — 21

11. Diamonds: Beauty, Resilience, And The Beauty Of Perspective — 24

12. The Key: Unlocking Perspectives — 28

13. The Window: A Portal Of Perspectives — 31

14. Beauty Standards Across The Globe — 34

15. The Silent Weight Of Beauty: A Journey Toward True Self-Love — 42

16. Letters To Imperfection — 51

17. Dear Crooked Teeth — 53

18. Dear Stretch Marks — 55

19. Dear Frizzy Hair — 57

20. Dear Big Nose — 59

21. Dear Acne — 61

22. Dear Aging Skin — 63

Contents

23. Dear Stutter — 65

24. Dear Overthinking — 67

25. Finding Beauty In My Flaws And Strengths — 69

26. Imperfect Fairy Tales: Love The Flaws Of A Perfect World — 73

27. The Sweetness Of Embracing Flaws — 77

28. Perfection Is Only A Story. — 79

29. Flaws Build Connection — 80

30. Authenticity Is Strength — 81

31. A Tale For Every Heart — 82

32. Cinderella: The Calloused-Handed Princess — 83

33. Snow White: The Princess Of The Unproportionate Smile — 88

34. Beauty And The Beast: A Love That Lasts — 92

35. A Day Without Beauty Standards — 96

36. Together, We Can Redefine The Beauty Of This World. — 102

37. WABI-SABI — 107

38. Kintsugi — 111

39. The Art Of Kintsugi: Repairing The Broken With Gold. — 115

40. Wabi-Sabi To Life — 118

41. The Heart Of Imperfection — 127

Imperfection is Perfection

Growing up as a brown-skinned, fat girl with huge glasses, I only wanted to fit into the labels. The labels that define the word pretty. Until one day, I realised the word "pretty" is all ours to define; it's society that compresses the windows of terms like "pretty" so much. To be accepted as a "pretty girl," you must look a certain way and wear certain clothes. All I ever ask is - Why these pre-decided norms?

To me, pretty is a girl's smile when confident in her skin. Today's world has raised beauty standards to an unachievable level. Young girls have started feeling immensely insecure about themselves because of all the fashion magazines and TV commercials showcasing a model with a perfect waist and skin. If only someone could show the efforts in hair and makeup and the lighting, the acne and dark circles hidden and covered under the makeup that lies above it, the efforts taken to edit out the perfect body and hide the stretch marks. It is all fake, and this fakeness seems natural to growing girls, and under all this, they forget the natural hormonal, the biological changes in a girl while her body changes. And now these girls are chasing a fake "perfect body," trying to make that a reality. This perfect image has promoted eating disorders among teens. Women have been stuck in the boxes of evolving societal beauty standards, trying to fit in and forgetting their true selves.There is nothing more rare, nor beautiful, than a woman who is unapologetically comfortable in her perfect imperfection, and that is the true essence of beauty.

A world without these so-called beauty standards would be my "Ideal World," promoting realism and acceptance of self. Beauty lies in individualism. Everyone is striving to achieve the hourglass figure; where is the uniqueness? Everyone is different and beautiful in their own way; this "own way" makes a person attractive. We live in a brainwashed generation. This world is full of sadness and anger, people trying to be what they are not. Media has consumed our heads, engulfed it with negativity.

CHAPTER TWO

Roses aren't always red,
And violets aren't exactly blue,
The society we live in
Never seems to speak the truth.

Smiles aren't always happy,
And frowns aren't always upset,
People are quick to judge,
And our feelings are what they forget.

Some people survive chaos
And that is how they grow
And some people thrive in chaos
Because chaos is all they know.

CHAPTER THREE

Beauty of Flaws

"A flaw"

This is how chat gpt, our own 'trusted' source of information and a lifesaver to many, defines " A flaw in a human",

"A flaw in a human is an imperfection or characteristic that deviates from societal norms of perfection, contributing to their unique individuality."

Notice how it said **"societal norms of perfection"**. Although the real question happens to be, What are these "societal norms of perfection"? And who makes these laws? The Government?

"Contributing to their own individuality". Flaws give you character. They make you different, unique. They make you an individual. Flaws come in all shapes and sizes, physical, mental, emotional, psychological, moral, social, cognitive and on and on and on.... They can be small, they can be big. Every flaw is different. In today's generation they are even classified into different types but they all have one thing in common. These flaws that you might hate, the ones you are trying to change, They make you who you are. They are a huge part of your personality and they all, each and every one of them are beautiful. They are not something to be feared or shunned, but instead celebrated and embraced. Stop striving for perfection and start embracing the beauty of imperfection.

The estimated population of the world is about 8 billion. If all of these 8 billion people start trying to be "perfect", start striving for one goal, which is fitting in the brackets of these societal norms, won't everyone just become the exact same person?

Recognise and Realise that nothing and I mean absolutely nothing in this world is perfect, or permanent. Be it your appearance, your relationships, your friendships, your success, your money and the examples are virtually endless. You like how you look today?It's amazing to be comfortable in your own skin, but will you still like how you look when you are bloated on your period one week from now? And that is what embracing is. Your relationship going well? That is great but does that mean there are no fights?. Fights dont fall under the "societal norms of perfect", but does that mean your relationship is not perfect for you?.

Perfect is a very subjective term, and the beauty of this word is that it is all yours to define. Make the most of this term. Instead of bending yourself to fit into this term, make it fit into you.

CHAPTER FOUR

In times without light,
Flaws become the stars that make the dark bright.
In places where stories are left untold,
Are where these imperfections unfold.

Stretch marks or a scars trace,
Become journeys or marks of grace.
The beauty of flaws, a truth to embrace.
In every imperfection, lies a gentle trace.

The imperfect, the pure, the raw,
Lies true beauty without a single flaw.
Beauty is not defined by any law,
It lies in everything I saw.

CHAPTER FIVE

Beauty lies in the Eyes of the Beholder

"Beauty lies in the eyes of the beholder", we have all heard this but have we really understood it?

This highlights the concept that states there is no universal standard for beauty. Beauty is whatever you make it to be. It is shaped by individual perspectives. Beauty of things exists merely in the mind. It is upon you to perceive it as beauty or ugliness.

Beauty lies in the eyes of the beholder, but the most liberating thing is realising that the beholder is you. Realising that beauty lies in undiscovered places and the most undiscovered area is always closest to you. It is you. Beauty lies in places inside yourself that you haven't even dared to take a peek in.

Beauty truly does exist in the eye of the beholder. It reflects how each person perceives and connects with the world. What one person sees as beautiful may not resonate with someone else, because beauty is deeply personal and shaped by individual experiences, emotions, and values. It's not just about physical appearances or the pre-decided societal norms that define attractiveness. Instead, it's about the moments, gestures, and qualities. May it be the warmth of a smile, the kindness in someone's eyes, the confidence in their walk or the grace in the way they carry themselves, beauty is something that each person defines for themselves. This unique perspective is what makes the concept of beauty so varied. It's as diverse as the people who experience it.

CHAPTER SIX

The Beauty of Perspectives.

What is a rose?

It can be viewed as a simple flower to people, but to poets and artists it is literally a form of information. Red roses usually suggest timeless love. So is it just a flower or a lot more?

The answer to that question really depends on how an individual perceives it to be.

Did you ever think that an inanimate object could teach us so many things?

A rose beautiful and tender petals and a stem full of thorns. As long as you are careful with it, handle it delicately you wont get poked.

A woman, a mesmerising woman, one with a gem of a soul but treat her poorly and see the inner thorns come out and make you bleed a river. This is what a rose teaches us. It teaches us to be our most alluring and elegant self, until someone messes with you, and when that happens stand up, speak up and unleash the devil. It reminds us to stop, pause and appreciate the little things in life. It teaches us to refrain from causing anyone any harm until they give you a reason to do otherwise, and when they do, unleash hell.

A rose reminds us that beauty frequently arises when grace and hardship are combined. It nudges us to treasure life's most beautiful moments with tender care, reminding us that they are delicate and transient. The rose, with its thorns, reminds us that true beauty is entwined with fragility and resilience, and that even the most alluring souls can conceal depths of strength and complexity. It calls us, in its bloom and withering, to recognize the impermanence in all things and to find beauty in the sunshine and thunder.

And yet, people say, a rose is just a flower.

This is the beauty of perception, the beauty of just a simple shift in mind. It can only be viewed with a deeper look.This planet is filled with beauty and magic, if only we take a step back to seek and cherish it.

CHAPTER SEVEN

Beauty lies in the eyes of the beholder,
But it is you who beholds this power.
It just takes eyes that are bolder,
To see that it is more than a flower.
Open your eyes,
The ones wide and kind.
It is not just a flower,
You will find.
In those eyes, a vision blooms,
A hidden world, where beauty looms.
Not in a clear-skinned face,
Not in the perfect hourglass shape,
But in the heart's own gentle grace.
Beauty's truth is softly told,
Only to those with heart's of gold,
Only those eyes will see,
The light within the mystery.
Beauty bends in every gaze,
In various forms and countless ways.
Ugly?, there is no such thing.
Look inside and see what wonders bring.
So let your eyes, your heart, your soul,
See the underlying beauty as a whole.
Because in the souls, where love resides,
True beauty never hides.

What is rain?

Rain? Is it the magical creation of nature or is it just simply an irritating season that makes your clothes dirty and muddy?

Some people see rain as a purifying force, washing away the old and bringing in the new, while the other half sees it as sadness and melancholy. Rain can also symbolise obstacles or challenges in life. It represents the challenges one must encounter for personal growth, but also the potential for overcoming these difficulties, much like how rain eventually gives way to clear sunny skies and soon the clouds disappear into the sky and the sun takes away the darkness shining light on the land again.

Rain can often symbolise pain and relief both at once. It depicts the release of pent up emotions showcasing both pain and the relief of getting over that pain and new beginnings. Like I said earlier, it is solely based on how one sees it. You can either learn to dance in it, or keep running from it.

Rain has always held a special place in our hearts. For some, it's a source of comfort; for others, chaos. But beyond these surface reactions, there's a deep and undeniable beauty to rain that resonates with us on a personal level, shaping our memories forever.It's as if the world slows down as rain pours above us, giving us a moment to pause and appreciate the little things nature has to offer. When I talk about rain I am immediately reminded of the 12 year old me, sitting by her window, watching raindrops race down the glass. Born and raised in the heart of Mumbai, I carry an undying love for the monsoon—a gift from my father. He refused to let me stay indoors, rushing me out into the rain with a childlike thrill, even as my mother's protests echoed behind us. Those fleeting moments, drenched in joy and rebellion, shaped my soul, filling it with the music of raindrops and the laughter of a carefree childhood. Rain manages to bring people closer, creating insignificant moments as special. It's no wonder why most love stories take place in the rain-it's a great setting that provides connection and warmth. On the other hand, it can take us to another world. There's a kind of magic in the way it changes our surroundings. That's the moment when our heads tend to wander and maybe see thoughts and ideas one could never imagine on such a bright day. But to people who love being creative in any form-artistic writing, or mere imagination-the rain is quite an inspiring muse that tends to open the door wide into limitless possibilities. Beauty lies in the gray area of blurring the real from the fantasy world, urging us to view the world before our eyes. Rain has a way of stirring memories, doesn't it? Raindrops pattering outside on the roof can bring it all back for a childhood: an afternoon spent indoors, snuggled and safe, watching the rain come down outside. Or it may remind us of some other place we once called home, where we'd go out the door and dance in the rain with it pouring on top of us and a clean, pure serenity took over.How we would jump in those dirty muddy puddles of water without thinking about the dirt and everything else in the world just disappeared. We stopped thinking and the fun was all that mattered to us, right there, in that moment we were living. When going down the slide became ten times more fun because the rain made us go faster, that is when we were truly living and appreciating the little moments of life. Somehow while growing up, we forget these little moments,we forget to appreciate them, to have fun and just truly enjoy.

CHAPTER EIGHT

Paradox of a Mirror

What is a mirror?

A reflective surface for some, plain, functional, and ordinary. But look deeper into the glass, and there's so much more to the story. It is a narrator, a silent witness, and a vessel for truth. The mirror holds the secrets, observes change, but does not itself change. Is it just a thing, or a gateway into self-reflection?

The choice is yours.

Did you ever think a piece of glass could reveal so much about who we are and who we pretend to be?

A mirror reflects our physical self, but it challenges us to look deeper. We often glance at it to fix our hair or straighten our clothes, but do we ever really see ourselves? The mirror is both brutally honest and endlessly kind. It reflects our flaws, yet never criticizes. It shows us our beauty, yet never boasts. It simply is.

And yet, its truth depends on perspective. A cracked mirror distorts reality, much like a fractured heart or a troubled mind. The same reflection can inspire pride in one person and insecurity in another. It's not the mirror that changes, but the viewer.

Think of the mirror as a metaphor for life. Life reflects what we project. Smile at it, and it smiles back. Frown, and the reflection darkens. The mirror teaches us accountability-it shows us that the way we view the world often mirrors the way we view ourselves. But a mirror has duality, much like the human soul. It is an instrument of clarity and illusion. It allows us to see ourselves yet never lets us truly touch what we see. It teaches us to question appearances and to understand that sometimes, what's reflected is not what's real.

A mirror, if looked at deeply, holds lessons. It teaches us to embrace our imperfections, to own our story, and to confront the truths we'd rather avoid. It reminds us that self-perception is powerful and that the way we see ourselves shapes the way we move through the world.

And yet, people say, a mirror is just glass.

This is the paradox of perspective, the gift of shifting our gaze. The world around us is full of lessons and wonder if only we pause to observe and reflect—quite literally.

CHAPTER NINE

The Silent Wisdom of a Candle

What is a candle?

In the first instance, a candle seems an utterly ordinary thing, an object to give light, a flame that flickers. But amidst this simplicity lies an enormous metaphor for life, resilience, and how the idea of fragility dances through the floorboards with strength. It is to truly embrace the power of perspective and see how one little humble object illuminates not just a room but so much more.It's delicate flame is capable of great force. A light breath can stifle it. It has in it the potential to drive off darkness, bring warmth to space, and a fire that shall set something aflame. At times, like all power, it doesn't roar but it whispers, it flickers with a soft and gentle glow-a presence without pomp.Think of how a candle transforms a room. Its light is different from the cold, clinical brightness of a bulb. It's softer, warmer, inviting stillness and introspection. A candle reminds us of the beauty of slowness, urging us to pause and embrace the quiet moments. It teaches us that even in a world obsessed with efficiency and speed, there is magic in the gentle, steady glow of something timeless.

A candle burns not for itself, but for others. In sacrifice, it finds warmth and gives light, devoting a portion of itself in order to create a path in the darkness. This selfless act reflects upon the beauty of generosity-the truth that sometimes one must give pieces of themselves for others to know their way.

But a candle's life is short. It reminds us of time passing, of life being fragile. Every flicker is a heartbeat, a moment slipping away. And in that transience lies its beauty. The candle teaches us to cherish the present, to see the brilliance of the flame while it burns, rather than lamenting its eventual end.

The wax of a candle tells its own story. Melting and dripping, it makes unique patterns—a proof of its journey. Each drop is a reminder that experiences in life are fleeting, yet they leave marks. The candle does not fight its melting; it accepts this as part of its purpose and teaches us to embrace our transformations.

The flame of a candle is never still. It dances, sways, and bends with the slightest draft. It mirrors life's unpredictability, showing us that even when the world shifts around us, we can continue to burn brightly. The candle's resilience lies in its ability to adapt to its environment, reminding us of our own capacity to endure and shine, even amidst uncertainty.

One candle can set another alight without losing any of its fire. This shared light speaks to how kindness and inspiration have no limit. One single gesture can bring out a lot of others to set the flame, creating ripple lights in this dark world of ours.

Darkness does not make the candle a hope. Its light, though very small, contains the promise of visibility, to find our way. A candle does not delete the darkness but coexists with it, giving contrast. It teaches us that light is not the absence of shadow but courage to glow in it.

But ritual and memory, as well as so much more, are candles interwoven with. For a birthday party or a mourning vigil, it allows space for the emotion to sit. There's often something specific that gets lit: a wish, a prayer, a remembrance. We are connected, quietly, through something greater than ourselves in that tiny flame.

Even in its extinguishing, a candle has something to teach. When the flame is blown out, a wisp of smoke rises, carrying with it the memory of light. It reminds us that endings, though inevitable, are not voids—they are transitions. The warmth lingers, the scent remains, and the space it illuminates is forever changed.

To see a candle is to see more than wax and wick; it is to see life itself. It is a symbol of resilience in the face of impermanence, of the quiet power of giving, and of the beauty found in moments of stillness. It teaches us to find light within ourselves and to share it freely, even when the world feels dark.

So the next time you light a candle, pause. Watch the flame dance. Feel its warmth. Let it remind you of the delicate balance between strength and fragility, and the extraordinary power of perspective to illuminate even the simplest things.

CHAPTER TEN

A Feather

What is a feather?

A feather is, at first glance, an unassuming object. Lightweight, delicate, often overlooked as it drifts to the ground. Yet, when we pause to truly consider it, the feather becomes a profound symbol—a reminder of resilience, freedom, and life's interconnectedness.There is a paradoxical beauty of a feather: it is so light that it can float while at the same time strong enough to lift a bird against gravity, able to ascend into the endless sky. Each feather is a master class in design—its barbs intricately aligned, its rachis a spine of quiet strength. A feather is never just a feather; it is a marvel of evolution, perfect union of function and grace.But the stories that feathers tell go much deeper than what is seen and touched. A feather is the icon of liberty. It pertains to the mastery of that which we humankind only imagine flying without an anchor to this earth. The act of holding a feather holds a piece of sky, a small fragment of something that has experienced the wind and defeated gravity.And yet, a feather is also, of course, a symbol of fragility. It can be plucked, torn, discarded, its purpose seemingly ended. But even then, it becomes something new—a token of beauty, a message of hope, a gift to the earth. Even in separation, there is a place for transformation of that feather.Each feather is unique. No two are the same, just as no two stories, dreams, or journeys ever are. The iridescent plume of the peacock tells of magnificence and allure that demands attention as it shimmers in the sun. The white feather of the swan whispers purity and grace, while having a quiet kind of beauty. Even the simplest feather of the sparrow speaks of resilience, a testament to survival amid chaos in life.

Feathers speak of balance too. For a bird, they are not ornaments but precision tools. A misplaced feather can make all the difference in a flight, just as a wrong step in life can make all the difference in the balance of things. Birds spend hours preening, taking care of their feathers. This is the lesson for us: to take care of ourselves, to cultivate those things that raise us up and to give up those things that no longer serve us.A feather dropped contains its own sense of wisdom. It is the emblem of growth and a reminder that even when lost, renewal begins. Birds do not shed their feathers in despair; they naturally remove the old for the new to take place. A feather on the ground isn't the end; it is a passage-a silent statement of how one moves forward, only by sometimes letting go.

Feathers have long been messengers in human culture. Finding a feather can feel serendipitous, as though the universe is whispering to us. To some, it is a sign of protection or a message from a loved one. To others, it symbolizes clarity, a nudge to rise above life's burdens and view challenges from a higher perspective.And then imagine the collective might of feathers. A single feather cannot lift a bird, but together, they create wings that lift to heights unbearably fantastic. This oneness reminds one of the power of unity—how small parts can be welded together to become something fantastic.

In the end, the feather is much more than an object. It's a metaphor for life's delicate balance of strength and fragility, beauty and function, freedom and grounding. It asks us to look beyond the surface, consider what we feel, and find the extraordinary in the ordinary.

So, the next time you see a feather, stop. Hold it in your hand. Trace its intricate lines. Feel its softness and its structure. Remember that it once rode the wind, touched the sky, and carried a life. And in that simple act of observation, let it remind you to rise above, to embrace your own flight, and to cherish the delicate yet resilient nature of existence.

CHAPTER ELEVEN

Diamonds: Beauty, Resilience, and the Beauty of Perspective

What is a diamond?

To one person, it could be that bright sparkling stone with the implications of wealth, love, or high status. Or it is only an arrangement of carbon atoms in crystallized forms created over millions of years. And yet, perspective brings forth to us what could be only termed as an end result, from pressure and changes, but that still exudes brilliance to an unattained height.

A diamond is formed in the darkness. It is born deep inside the Earth, where heat and pressure merge in a form that's simply unimaginable, pushing carbon atoms into a rigid lattice. The conditions that seem destructive are exactly those which create something special. That process gives us the message that even under extreme pressure, beauty and strength could emerge. Challenges are not obstacles; they are opportunities for transformation.It's the journey of a diamond-to-be, showing a strong will in a world so violent. Its trip from core to surface and beyond is just so full of time, earthquakes, and excavations. The cutting and polishing make it try, but every fine cut helps make it sparkle. A diamond shows us that those sharp edges in life—moments that form us—are the things that refine us to become something extra.It's not clear whether clarity is its beauty or a sign of it; tiny inclusions within a diamond, considered defects, are instead records of how it formed. Imperfections in the diamond don't diminish its value but rather add character by reminding one that perfection isn't the absence of flaws but that it shines bright despite them.A diamond refracts light, capturing even the most faint beam of light and dispersing it in all directions to cast rainbows in every way. The nature of this refraction represents multifaceted views of perspective; as with the diamond, a single stone that displays hues at different angles of observation, similarly does life for the way that we want to view it display varied truths.Its durability should be considered—diamonds are among the hardest natural substances on Earth. Such strength is a metaphor for resilience, the ability to stand against time and adversity without losing integrity. It reminds us that even the smallest, seemingly fragile things can hold immense power when they are shaped by patience and perseverance.

The value of the diamond will also rely on human perception. A rough diamond, uncut and unpolished, might seem ordinary to the naked eye, whereas its potential was only acknowledged by vision and craftsmanship. This teaches us that beauty often lies hidden, waiting for someone to recognize and nurture it.

In relationships, a diamond has become a symbol of commitment and eternity. The exchange of a diamond ring signifies love's enduring nature, a promise to weather life's pressures together. Yet, beyond romance, a diamond can symbolize any bond forged through shared trials—a friendship, a family, a partnership.

Diamonds also have a deeper truth to them: because they are rare, they are precious. They remind us of the importance of valuing the rare in our lives: true connections, brief moments of happiness, and what makes us special. They tell us to care for these treasures, hold them close, and celebrate their brilliance.

But a diamond's story is not without controversy. The diamond trade has been a source of conflict, exploitation, and environmental harm. This darker facet challenges us to confront the ethical implications of our desires. It teaches us that beauty cannot truly shine unless it is accompanied by integrity and mindfulness.

A diamond is more than just an object-it is a paradox. It is old, yet it is timeless. It is hard, yet it is delicate. It is simple in its makeup, yet infinitely complex in its creation. The value of the diamond is not only in the physical properties that it has, but in what we attribute meaning to it, in the stories it tells, and in the lessons it gives.

The next time you gaze at a diamond, think not only about the sparkle but also about the depth from where it comes, the forces that shaped it, and the hands that brought out the brilliance. It should remind you of your own path-you who can persevere, transform, and shine. For in all facets of a diamond, there lies a testament to the beauty of resilience, the power of perspective, and infinite potential within each of us.

CHAPTER TWELVE

The Key: Unlocking Perspectives

What is a key?

A key is an unremarkable object to most—small, cold, forged from metal, and often tucked away in a pocket or forgotten in a drawer. But when seen through the lens of perspective, the key becomes a symbol of possibility, a bridge between limitation and liberation, a silent witness to the moments of access and transformation in our lives.

What is a key but a promise? It brings within its form the ability to open, to unlock, to let in. A locked door is an impassable barrier—enigmatic and fearful—but a key to hand makes that identical door into a possibility. The key teaches that there are times when we are stumbling over mountains not because they cannot be climbed but simply because we do not approach from the right angle, with the right implement, or in the right spirit.

A key is also a symbol of trust. When you give your key to someone, you give them access—to your home, your car, or a part of your life. It is a gesture of faith, a tangible representation of connection. Yet, the key also reminds us of boundaries—it can lock just as easily as it unlocks. It shows us the duality of human relationships, the need for both openness and protection.

Think of a key: its grooves, ridges, and cuts. No two are the same. Every key is shaped to fit one lock exactly, reminding us that solutions are not one-size-fits-all. The beauty of the key lies in its individuality, a testament to the uniqueness of every problem, every opportunity, and every person.

The act of turning a key is small, almost imperceptible, but the consequences can be huge. A turn of a key can open the gates of a garden, unlock a safe filled with treasures, or start an engine that carries you to new destinations. This small action teaches us that even the simplest gestures, the quietest decisions, can lead to monumental changes.A forgotten key is frustrating, reminding one of how small things can hold so much power. Yet, a lost key usually leads to finding something new: a hidden passage, an alternative route, or a locksmith who creates a new one altogether. The loss of a key teaches us resilience, that even when access is denied, ingenuity can create new paths.Keys carry history too. An old skeleton key, rusty and worn, speaks of the good old days—of locks that do not exist anymore, doors that no longer stand. Such keys are relics that speak of places, people, and secrets. It reminds one that access is not always a present thing; it can be to dig out the past and learn from it.

Symbolism of keys is deeply rooted in culture and

literature. They signify freedom, such as a cell-door key or shackles key, and symbolize wisdom, such as knowledge's key. Keys have often been used to symbolize hidden truths, treasure, and forbidden realms. They remind us that what we seek is often locked away, waiting for us to discover the means to unlock it.

And then, there is the idea of being "the key." In relationships, careers, or challenges, we often find that we ourselves hold the answers we seek. The key reminds us to look inward, to trust our own instincts, and to believe in our ability to unlock the doors of opportunity and understanding.Even a keyring, a set of keys, speaks about roles and the number of places we have to be in or hold; the various responsibilities we have and the lives we touch. Each key on that ring is a thread connecting us to a place, a person, or a purpose.But the deepest lesson of the key is this: not all doors are meant to be opened. Some locks protect us, keeping us safe from harm. Some doors remain closed, not as barriers, but as reminders to focus on the paths already unlocked. The key teaches us discernment—the ability to know which doors to pursue and which to leave untouched.

Next time you hold a key, stop for a moment. Feel the weight in your hand, the grooves under your fingers. Reflect on what power it possesses: to change not just a doorway, but a moment, a day, a life. The key is more than a tool; it's a reminder of potential, a testament to transformation, and a beautiful viewpoint.

CHAPTER THIRTEEN

The Window: A Portal of Perspectives

What is a window?

For many, it's a pane of glass, a frame within a wall to let in light and air. When viewed through the lens of perspective, a window becomes a metaphor of deep and profound import as we go through life, an unseen witness to the dance of our inner and outer worlds.A window is the very thing of clarity and division. It makes us see the world, while keeping us separate from it. We can peer through it and see life's chaos and beauty without being tossed into its storm. But is the window, then, our protector from what lies outside or our prison, confining us within? The magic of perspective is that one way or another, it's a matter of choice.

A fogged window is a call to action for us to clear away the moisture so we may see again. It teaches us that clarity isn't something automatically granted; rather, it's something we work for. On the other hand, a broken window reminds us of vulnerability. The strongest barriers break and leave one exposed to elements.Its beauty lies in what it frames out. A sun rising through that window is the light spilling into a room, but even more, an instant of marvel, a possibility of infinite that is painted against the hues of orange and pink. The window presents a different scene at dusk—one of a silent world fading in darkness, reminding one of something coming to end and resting down.

Windows also reveal our emotional moods. They are the gateways to possibilities when the sun is shining bright. We feel urged to step outside and into the world. During rainy days, they are like shields from where we observe the storm raging within our view yet safely in ourselves. The raindrops on the windowpane reflect tears or even whispers of nostalgia, reminding us that nature has an intimate relationship with emotions.

But a window is not about seeing out-only. It's also about seeing in. From outside, it looks like a glimpse of someone else's world, perhaps an image or two of somebody's life caught under a lone lightbulb or behind pulled curtains. This is a reminder of the unseen lives we walk by every day, full of stories.Finally, there is this magical power in opening a window. The movement of fresh breeze is an invitation to change. It teaches man that sometimes it is necessary to let go of stale air to have room for the new.

Yet, even a closed window can teach us. It offers us reflection, literally and metaphorically. As you stand before it, the world outside merges with your own image. It's a reminder that what we see is always influenced by who we are. The window does not change, but our perception of it does.

A window's perspective changes with time and season. In the morning, it's a gateway to beginnings; at night, it transforms into a mirror, showing us the darkness outside and the light within. In spring, it bursts with life—a view of blooming flowers and singing birds. In winter, it frames a quiet, snow-covered world, inviting introspection and stillness.

Then, of course, there is the ultimate shift in perspective: crossing through the window. For so long, it may have felt like a barrier, separating us from the world beyond. But the moment we fling it wide and cross its threshold, the window ceases to be a frame and becomes a bridge. It shows us that barriers are often illusions, that the only thing holding us back is our willingness to step forward.

The window is simple, but it holds within it profound truths. It teaches us to see the world not as it is but as it could be. It reminds us that perspective is not static; it shifts with light, mood, and time. And it calls us to pause, to really look, and to recognize that even the most ordinary objects can become extraordinary when viewed with an open mind.

In the end, a window is more than just a pane of glass—it's a reflection of life itself. It shows us that the way we frame the world defines the way we live in it.

CHAPTER FOURTEEN

Beauty standards across the globe

Cultural Differences in Beauty Standards

Let's start with cultural differences.

In countries like China, Japan, and Korea, pale skin has been prized for centuries. This started because, back then pale skin was a sign of wealth and status. Being pale meant you weren't out working in the fields. This preference continues today, with many people avoiding the sun or using skin-lightening products to obtain a lighter complexion.Historically, it's because poor people had to work outside in the sun. Farmers get tan and have dark skin. It's a sign of being lower class if you're forced to do manual labour to survive. Rich people can be inside, out of the sun and study and do more white collar jobs. If you're light-skinned, it's a sign of being upper class that your job doesn't require you to be outside all day. Back in the day, being "white-skinned" was associated with social status and wealth.

In ancient China, it was customary for ladies of higher

social standing to bind their feet in the shape of a lotus, with the requirement that they be around three inches in length. Once again, these were a symbol of status as only women who could afford to not work the fields could have their feet bound. This ensured that, from a young age, women would stay inside and be docile, training to be the perfect housewife for their future husband. In addition, they were used as a measure of how desirable a woman was as the tiny, covered.Footbinding usually began when girls were between 4 and 6 years old; some were as young as 3, and some as old as 12. Mothers, grandmothers, or older female relatives first bound the girl's feet. The ultimate goal was to make them 3 inches long, the ideal "golden lotus" foot, though few individuals actually achieved that goal. The four smaller toes were tucked underneath, pulled toward the heel, and wrapped with bandages. Each time the feet were unbound, the bandages and feet were cleaned. Any dead skin, blisters, dried blood, and pus were removed. The process could cause paralysis, gagerine, ulceration, or death, though death was rare. Binding the feet continued for the rest of the girl's life. Decorative shoes and leggings were worn over the bandages and could differ with the time of day and occasion.

In Ancient Japan, women's beauty standards varied greatly. Much like China, round chins and wide shoulders were admired, because, similarly, being plumper was a symbol of wealth. What is interesting, however, is that there are many Japanese beauty standards that seem to be in direct opposition to Chinese beauty standards. During Japan's Heian period, long hair was valued among women, perhaps in opposition to China's trend of short hair and updos at that time. Unlike Chinese women who were expected to have certain skills of a diligent housewife, a Japanese woman's beauty could be augmented through her ability to sing; women who had the ability to sing were perceived as more beautiful than those that couldn't. In addition, the picture of docility was not always revered in Japanese beauty; during the Kamakura period, strong and active women were looked up to rather than those who stayed at home. Slowly, this extravagant use of makeup and fashion died down to a more natural faced trend. Cosmetic sales continued to soar, however, as makeup was now used to help women achieve this natural, clean faced, innocent look.

Korea valued a round face and thin lips influenced by the role of status. While beauty was a symbol of status in China and Japan, it was even more so in Korea. Women of the upper class would always have their hair well kept and makeup on. Those in lower classes also did so but were unable to do so to the same calibre. In addition, it was believed that good souls were held in beautiful bodies. As a result, women always made sure that they looked their best. After the discovery of lead powder, the creation of cosmetics became much easier and much more extravagant. As a result, Koreans became obsessed with cosmetics and beauty.

The Korean culture surrounding cosmetics was able to spread across the ocean to China.

In the early 1900s, Asian beauty standards began to shift due to increased interaction with Western nations and increased industrialization. Narrow eyes began to fall out of favour in exchange for large eyes with double eyelids and round faces were overlooked in favour of sharp, delicate structures that were common among Americans and Europeans. The makeup products offered in Korea became much more numerous, most likely due to the increased industrialization. Unlike earlier in history, there was much more similarity between the beauty standards of each culture; the Koreans borrowed much of their standards from Japan so the women of the two countries had very similar looks. Though makeup became much more accessible to different groups of people, it was still a sign of status as only those rich enough and those with enough time could make sure to do their hair and makeup well everyday.

Despite the slight effects of Hollywood on Asian beauty standards in the early half of the 1900s, it was not until after the Second World War that they took full effect. In light of world politics, capitalism became desirable so women would try to make themselves look westernised. American makeup products such as mascara and oil based foundations became much more prevalent in people's normal routines. Asians began to keep up with the beauty standards in America and based all their looks off of that. While the spread of ideas is very useful in some cases, it was not here. Since Western features were so popular, women of all ages would go to extremes to achieve them. They would get their hair done very often, try to stay out of the sun for status and to appear white, and find ways to make their features look more American. In a sense, girls were being told that their natural features were not enough and that if they wanted to be considered "beautiful", they had to conform to Western standards of beauty.

Meanwhile, beauty standards in China and North Korea were very different. Since the collective and hard work were celebrated, tan and strong individuals who were all dressed in very similar colours, the opposite of what was valued in Ancient China, were praised. Everyone wore a uniform of very the same colours everyday and there was not a lot of makeup lying around. Despite this, women found ways to express themselves through their hair.

Today, K-beauty is one of the most popular beauty standards both in the Asian world and in the Western world. Beautiful, slim girls with tiny waists, large eyes, long brown hair, double eyelids, delicate bone structure, and pale skin are revered. Though this standard is so different from the one present in East Asia 500 years ago, it still carries many of the same cultural connotations with it. The large eyes, delicate bone structure, and pale skin that are so sought after create an image of delicacy and innocence much like the bound feet and narrow eyes did in Ancient China.

This new beauty standard remains to evolve; the stereotype about women sitting pretty in their homes is now fading. Generation after generation of women across all cultures have borne the weight of expectations that put the definition of their identity upon how they look, as though their value lay in being weighed and measured against someone else's appraisal. And now, here we are-at the crossroads of old ideas crumbling and new ones forming. But with all the advancement, beauty and privilege are interwoven; there will always be classes.

The celebrated ones are the ones who have the means to change themselves into the new molding perfection. Those without the means fall into obscurity, called "less beautiful" by a judging society that takes little time to pass judgment on people. That is not merely a matter of appearance; it is a question of power: whose voices count and whose don't. It is a system that promotes inequality in ways we don't always recognize. Beauty should not be a currency for worth. It should not divide us into those who belong and those who don't.

It's time for us,as a global community, to break free from the shackles of ancient beauty standards that were born from a time when women were treated as second-class citizens, their worth tied to their ability to please others. It's time to embrace a world where women can define beauty on their own terms, free from the weight of external expectations. Women should feel the liberty to be proud of the natural beauty she possesses—or embellish it if desired—not to match another's expectations but to suit her own.

Beauty standards all over the world are not unchangeable; they are flexible, dynamic, and in motion. What a beauty standard considers beautiful today will probably be opposite tomorrow. This is the great variability, and an important truth: beauty isn't absolute; it's a reflection of the society and time we live in. This means realizing that giving into such an excessively high standard's flaws will gradually become perceivable. We can then find freedom in the knowledge that beauty is a construct, not a rule.

Beauty is deep-seated interwoven with culture, history, and the social forces of our lives. It varies widely across societies, time periods, and social classes. Those standards of beauty, when closely examined, tell us powerful stories about values, beliefs, and even the economic conditions of a culture. For example, in Asia, we have centuries of history that have left us with beauty ideals rooted in traditions that once sought to keep women in defined roles—silent, submissive, and ornamental. But beauty, at its core, should not be a weapon to control or define anyone.

The heart of the issue lies in how we view beauty: as a fixed measure or as a fluid, diverse expression of individuality. Imagine a world where beauty isn't privileged or perfect, but a laughter-filled moment, or the lines written by wisdom of years, or the glint in a person's eye as they come to life when being passionately alive. Imagine a world in which we instruct our daughters that their minds and hearts are the most precious aspects of their worth before we remind them how to look.

It takes all of us to shatter these narrow definitions of beauty handed down to us. We should celebrate diversity not as a trend but as the truth that represents the richness of our humanity. We should remind ourselves—and each other—that beauty is not something earned, bought, or compared; it simply exists in every one of us, in different ways and forms.

It is only when we stop trying to fit into someone else's ideal of beauty that we make room for something far more meaningful: authenticity. And in that space, we can finally begin to see ourselves—and one another—as we truly are, beyond the filters and the expectations. That is where the real beauty lies.

Let this be the generation that buries the requirement of conformity and instead embarks on our lives with unapologetic individuality. Let this be the moment when we redefine beauty from trying to measure it or mold it but as celebrating the many ways in which we exist in this world.

CHAPTER FIFTEEN

The Silent Weight of Beauty: A Journey Toward True Self-Love

Beauty is a word that carries weight—a weight that is not only physical but deeply emotional, psychological, and cultural. In a world obsessed with outward appearances, beauty has been reduced to a checklist of attributes, a series of boxes to tick off in order to feel seen, worthy, or even loved. The struggle to meet those standards starts so young that by the time we are adults, we are already deeply entangled in the complex web of expectations, comparisons, and self-doubt.

For as long as I can remember, beauty was always the thing I needed to "work on." Not just as something that came naturally, but as something I had to perfect. It was never about looking pretty in a photo or wearing the right makeup. It was the soft, constant whisper that I needed to change to be loved. That who I was—naturally—wasn't enough. The world told me that if I wanted to be seen, wanted to be valued, I had to become something else. Something flawless. Something perfect.I remember the first time I ever felt ugly. I was 12 years old, just on the edge of adolescence, when a comment was made about my appearance. I can still hear it as clearly as if it were yesterday. "You have a beautiful face, but you're too dark for people to really notice." And later, when I became a bit older, I was told, "You're beautiful, but you're just a little too big for people to take you seriously." Those words struck me like a thunderclap, sending a ripple of shame through my entire body. The words did not hold malice but ignorance; they sprang from centuries of social conditioning. The fact that my natural skin color—something I had no say in—and my body—something I never felt ashamed of—were somehow beneath something, somehow undeserving of notice or adoration, stuck to me.

From that moment forward, I began to view myself in a new light: I wasn't a child anymore; I became a project. I learned to use makeup to alter my facial structure, learn to hide my skin, learn how to dress so as not to draw attention to what God created. I learned how to diet, how to avoid food, how to "shrink" myself to fit a mold. I learned that beauty wasn't something that came easily—it was something to be worked for, to be earned, to be created.

Every mirror became a battleground. Every reflection was a reminder that I was never quite perfect. There was always something to fix, something to hide, something to change. Each and every time I applied a layer of foundation, or contoured my face just right, I was trying to bury a little piece of myself. A little piece of my true self. And each time I covered up, I felt like I was becoming more and more distant from the person I was meant to be.

Then came the moment when I decided to lose weight. The world told me I had to. I could feel people judging me in every mirror through which I was passing, or every time that I went outside, or everyone around me; it was a feeling of a body that belongs to no one, a feeling of a body that does not measure up. This is why, I did all that I was doing: began losing the weight I had gained in the first place. Slowly the numbers on that scale started to shrink. I pushed myself, restricted my food, counted calories. At first, I felt proud. I felt like I was finally fitting into the mold I had spent my whole life trying to fit into.

But as the pounds melted away, something strange happened. The compliments started rolling in. "You look amazing! You've lost so much weight, you look like a new person! I basked in them, like words could make up for all the years of self-doubt, like being thin will be the answer to my struggle. And yet, when I look in the mirror today, I feel I'm not good enough. Still the same fat girl under my skin when I stare at myself with my eyes.". The same woman who had always felt less than, who had always felt worthless. And the worst part? People started saying things like, "Oh my God, are you okay? You look so skinny!Do you live on air?

The comments came from all sides—first, it was "you're too big," and then, after losing weight, it was "you're too skinny." It was as though no matter what I did, I would never get it right.". When I was fat, they asked me to lose weight. When I lost weight, people said I was too lean. The world never stopped telling me I should change.

And thus, as the scale continued to plummet, I couldn't help but feel that I wasn't enough. I felt like I was stuck in some kind of infinite loop of dissatisfaction, searching for a version of myself that was always unattainable. I recall my first experience walking into a party without wearing any makeup, no tricks, no fashion statement to hide behind. It was bold, but desperate, at the same time; I just reached a point where I was so exhausted with the performance. Tired of trying to fit in a version of beauty that was not mine in the first place. I walked into that room, and eyes were upon me. It wasn't the kind I had always desired, which is admiration and affection, but that awkward, intruding stare.

It was like I was an alien in the room.

I could feel my cheeks on fire with judgment, and insecurity crawled beneath my skin, whispering to me, "You should have stayed home; you should have kept the mask on, hid the parts of me I thought the world could not love.". The shame was complete, but it wasn't until later, when I was standing alone in front of a mirror, all that grime washed away and streaming down, that I felt something different. Something I had never felt before. The first flicker of freedom. There, in the silence of my room, I realized I had been running my whole life—running from who I was, running from the very things that made me me. I was chasing a standard of beauty that wasn't just foreign to me—it was suffocating me. I had built walls around myself, convinced that if I could just be perfect, the world would love me.

But what I learned that night was that perfection was a

trap. It was a mask, a cloak, something I wore to protect myself from the fear that maybe, just maybe, I wasn't enough. What is it that makes us believe we are not enough? Who are we living for when we spend our time chasing beauty that the world tells us is worth pursuing?

Who are we trying to impress, and why do we place our sense of worth in the hands of people who will never truly see us, never truly know us?

The truth is, when we spend so much time trying to please the world, we lose touch with the person who deserves to be loved the most—the person looking back at us in the mirror. We learned that beauty was something you earned. It's something that's hard work, something that you can work at, craft, perfect. And the more I sought after beauty in those places I had been told to look for it—through routines, skincare, the perfect selfie—the more it seemed to slink away, like a snake disappearing into dust. It felt like a wind chase; you never could catch it, always thought you would feel complete when you caught it. But beneath all that anxiety of being "too dark" and the ache of feeling fat was the ongoing fight against my body. I wasn't done being inadequate even when I had lost the weight; the world still weighed upon me in another guise. When I was fat, I was too big. When I got thin, I was too skinny. And so I found myself trapped in the cycle, always wondering when I would be enough.It dawned on me: no matter how much I changed, no matter how much I shrunk or sculpted, it would never be enough, because the expectation had never been about me at all.It had always been about fitting into a mold that was designed for someone else. But this belief is a lie. The truth I started to see—slowly, painfully—was that beauty isn't a product. It's not a look, it's not a trend, it's not something that can be created with makeup or filtered through an app. Beauty is the act of allowing yourself to exist without apology.It's the rawness of being real, accepting every wrinkle, every scar, every inch of fat, for these things are not mistakes, but parts of the story that we tell through our lives. They tell the world who we are and where we have been and how beautifully human we truly are. There was a moment – a fleeting, fragile moment when I let go of all layers, all filters, all masks to be seen. I stood in front of that mirror, with nothing to hide, and for the first time in my life, I saw myself as I truly was—not someone who needed to be fixed, but someone who was whole.And in that moment, I realized how deeply I had been lying to myself all these years.The beauty I had been chasing had always been inside me, waiting to be acknowledged.But it's so much easier to hide. It's easier to put on the mask and pretend to be what the world wants us to be. It's easier to be perfect, to be polished, to be "flawless" because in that perfection, we believe we are safe. But safety is not worth the cost of losing yourself.

And yet, how many of us run after this ever-elusive illusion? How many of us gauge ourselves according to their measures? How many of us continue believing if only we did it, just right; or if we look a little more put together, a little prettier, people would love us? The truth is, we already are. We are already worthy. Not because we are perfect, not because we fit some arbitrary ideal of beauty, but because we are real. Our faces, our bodies, our scars—these are all part of our story, and they are all worth loving. There is nothing more beautiful than the truth. There is nothing more powerful than showing up as who you are, unapologetically, unafraid. The next time you look into the mirror, I hope that you see something more than yourself. I hope you see someone who has lived, who has loved, felt joy and sadness, and overcomes every obstacle in life. And I hope that you will be a person who deserves love exactly the way you are because you are beautiful. You have always been beautiful, in every way that matters. And once you realize that, you'll never need to look for beauty anywhere else again.

Redefining 'Beauty Standards'.

Understanding that beauty standards are always changing is like understanding the seasons—they come and go, bringing something new each time. Beauty standards are not set in stone, nor are the rules of these so called "beauty standards" engraved somewhere where you are obligated to follow these standards and fit in all the boxes.What's considered beautiful today might not be in a few years, and that's okay. It gives you the space to appreciate who you are right now, without feeling like you need to keep up with trends that are shifting constantly.

Think about how fashion changes over time, what was trendy in the '90s might look outdated today, and the same goes for beauty. Let's take skinny jeans for an example, they were extremely popular around the mid 2000's, although they started gaining traction and were a major trend around the 2010's.They were embraced by both men and women as a fashion staple.While they dominated the fashion community for over a decade, their popularity has declined in the recent years, with looser-fitting styles like 'mom jeans', 'straight-leg jeans', and 'wide-leg pants' gaining more attention by the consumers. And slowly and steadily the 'skinny jeans' trend has started to fade away, while a new fashion trend takes over.

By knowing this, you can be more at peace with yourself, understanding that there's no single way to be beautiful and that the word beauty is highly subjective. This awareness is meant to help you stop comparing yourself to others because you understand that everyone's idea of beauty is influenced by where and when they grew up, and what they've been exposed to.This understanding also helps you embrace diversity in beauty. If you're aware that standards are not the same everywhere or for everyone, it becomes easier to appreciate different types of beauty. You stop looking for one "right" way to look and start seeing the beauty in the variety of people around you. It also encourages you to challenge the status quo, supporting more inclusive and realistic representations of beauty that reflect real people, not just the narrow ideals we're often sold.

On a deeper level, when you see that beauty standards are shaped by society and industries, it opens your eyes to the fact that a lot of these ideals are created to sell products. **Companies often push certain looks or trends because it's profitable, not because they're universally better or more beautiful.** We are living in a money making,brainwashed generation primarily focussing on profits and success.These companies will make you believe anything to gain profits.Once you see that, you can start to detach your self-worth from those changing standards and focus more on what makes you feel unique, special and authentic.Even though we live in a society that often equates success with money, you still have the power to define success on your own terms. You still have the power to define beauty on your own terms. You have the power to make the box designed for you to fit in instead of trying to fit in a rigid box that isn't meant for you in the first place.

CHAPTER SIXTEEN

Letters to Imperfection

Chapter 1: Dear Freckles

Dear Freckles,

I once cursed the sun for having made you rise alive on my cheeks. A child, I used to scrub my face raw to get the dirt out of me. They would constantly mock me at school, calling you "splattered paint" or "spots gone wrong." The words stuck, and I saw you as an accident, a blemish that set me apart in all the wrong ways. I wished for smooth, spotless skin like the models in magazines.

I spent so many summers hiding from the sun, trying to keep you at bay. But you returned every year, unyielding, defiant, like little constellations blooming across my skin. And then came the boy—the first person who saw you differently. He traced you with his fingertips, calling you stars and me the night sky. I blushed, and for the first time, I felt beautiful.

Now, I see you for what you really are: the map of all the summers I lived under open skies, the proof of every laugh, every carefree moment I didn't think twice about.

You are golden ink, writing my story on my skin, each spot a memory of warmth and joy. You remind me that beauty doesn't have to fit into a box; it can be irregular, untamed, and unapologetic.

I am sorry for the years I tried to erase you. Now, I embrace you as part of me—a part I wouldn't trade for anything.

Love,
Me

CHAPTER SEVENTEEN

Dear Crooked Teeth

Dear Crooked Teeth,

You have always been obstinate, haven't you? And I've spent years hiding you behind tight-lipped smiles, ashamed of how you wouldn't conform to the straight, perfect teeth I envied in others. I loathed how you made me feel different, like I wasn't a part of the world of perfectly symmetrical grins.

Braces came and went, years of discomfort spent trying to make you fit the mold. But you resisted, holding your ground, as if to say, "This is who I am." I resented you for your defiance, for refusing to change despite my efforts.

And then, one day, I saw a photograph of myself laughing. It wasn't the careful, practiced smile I'd mastered but a genuine, unguarded moment of joy. There you were, in full view—crooked, unapologetic, and undeniably mine. That's when it hit me: you weren't the problem. My fear was.

You are the reason my smile stands out, the reason it's mine and no one else's. You're a reminder that perfection isn't necessary for beauty, that individuality is far more captivating. You've taught me to embrace the things that make me different, to celebrate the uniqueness that sets me apart.

So thank you, dear Crooked Teeth, for being yourself even when I could not. You have taught me that beauty is not in conformity; it is in authenticity.

Forever yours,
Me

CHAPTER EIGHTEEN

Dear Stretch Marks

Dear Stretch Marks,

For so long, I saw you as a map to nowhere. I stared at you in the mirror with frustration, tracing your silvery lines with a mix of shame and resentment. You reminded me of changes I didn't ask for—growth spurts that came too fast, weight gained and lost, transitions I wasn't ready to embrace.

I covered you up, hid you under long sleeves, high-waisted jeans, and swimsuits that never saw the light of day. I pleaded with you to disappear, searching for creams and remedies that promised to erase you. I thought you were a sign of weakness, a flaw I had to fix.

One day, I watched a friend trace the stretch marks on her pregnant belly with reverence. She called them "lightning strikes," proof that her body had carried life, that it had stretched and grown to create something extraordinary. In that moment, I began to see you differently—not as blemishes, but as art.

You are my story, etched into my skin. Each line speaks

of resilience, of a body that has grown, adapted, and endured. You are proof of how hard I've been on myself and how strong I've had to be. You remind me that beauty isn't in flawless perfection but in the marks of a life lived fully.

Thus, dear Stretch Marks, I no longer view them as imperfections. They are victories; they are proof of my journey, and I'm learning to wear them proudly.

Thanks,

Me

CHAPTER NINETEEN

Dear Frizzy Hair

Dear Frizzy Hair,

How many hours have I spent trying to tame you? Straighteners, serums, gels, and sprays—all in a desperate attempt to make you behave. You rebelled every time, springing back to your wild, untamed self as if to say, "This is who I am." I hated your defiance. I wanted you to be sleek and smooth, like the glossy hair I saw in commercials.

I ironed you into submission; drowning you under product after product, hoping that is where you'll finally submit, but what only resulted was that the damage had built up on your beauty and took away my views of your essence.

It took a rainy day for me to see you in a new light. The rain brought you back to life, letting your natural curls spring free. A stranger stopped me that day and said, "Your hair is so alive, so full of character." For the first time, I saw you for what you are: unapologetic, untamed, and uniquely mine.

Now, I do not fight with you anymore; I learned how to work with you, to welcome your wildness instead of controlling it. You remind me that beauty doesn't have to be polished and perfect; it could be raw, real, and free.

Therefore, dear Frizzy Hair, thanks for teaching me to let go of control and embrace the beauty of imperfection. You are not unruly; you are alive, just like me.

Warm regards,
Me

CHAPTER TWENTY

Dear Big Nose

Dear Big Nose,

You were the bane of my adolescence. I compared you to the button noses of my classmates, wishing you were smaller, cuter, less conspicuous. I avoided profile photos, convinced you took up too much space. You made me feel like I didn't belong in a world that idolized delicate, dainty features.

Then I went to visit my grandmother in India, and everything changed. She looked at me with pride and said, "You have the nose of our ancestors—strong, proud, and regal." She told me it symbolized resilience and connection to the women who came before me. I stopped seeing you as "too big" and began to see you as just right.

You are my heritage, my identity. You carry the stories of generations, a testament to where I come from and who I am. You remind me that beauty isn't about fitting into narrow standards—it's about owning what makes us unique.

So, dear Big Nose, forgive me for the years I wished you

were different. Now I know you are not a flaw, but a feature to be proud of. You are my strength, my story, and I would not trade you for anything.

Proudly,
Me

CHAPTER TWENTY-ONE

Dear Acne

Dear Acne,

You were my unwanted companion, appearing at the most inconvenient times. Initially, you seemed harmless- a few blemishes I thought would disappear with age. But you lingered, carving your presence into my skin and my confidence. You made me avoid mirrors, dodge photographs, and shrink under the scrutiny of others. Every morning, I would wake up dreading your latest display, wishing you away with creams, treatments, and desperate prayers.

You've scarred my face so much; it reminds you of wars lost on its own scars. You also hurt me so deeply—not by physical inflammation caused by your hurting, but it pained to think I'm never enough and more so hurt. I blame you for these flaws on me: unappealing and, even worse, depriving of carefree shining brightness.

But as time went by, I began to see you differently. You forced me to redefine beauty—not as flawless perfection but as authenticity. You taught me patience and how to prioritize self-care, not just for my skin but for my soul.

The scars you left are no longer signs of defeat; they are proof of survival. They remind me that I am more than my appearance, that my worth is not skin-deep.

So, Acne, dear one I no longer see you as my adversary but as a teacher. You taught me to love the imperfections that make me human and find beauty in resilience. I never thought that true confidence wasn't about having perfect skin but rather loving the one you are in.

DISCLAIMER- This does in no way mean I want you to come back, it just means I have stopped despising you. You are natural, and this is how I should have looked at you in the first place.

Yours sincerely,
Someone learning to glow from within

CHAPTER TWENTY-TWO

Dear Aging Skin

Dear Aging Skin,

You came slowly, so quietly that I almost didn't notice. A faint line here, a gentle crease there—signs of time making its mark. At first, I resented you. The smoothness of my youth felt like it was slipping away, and I wasn't ready to let it go. I chased every cream, serum, and promise of reversing the inevitable, hoping to turn back the clock.

But then, I started to look closer. Those fine lines around my eyes aren't flaws; they are the echoes of a thousand laughs shared with loved ones. The creases in my forehead tell the story of moments spent pondering life's mysteries. Even the softening of my skin is a gentle reminder of the years I've lived, the storms I've weathered, and the joys I've celebrated.

You are not betrayal, Aging Skin. You are the history of my life written on texture and tone. You teach me wisdom that I have gathered, experiences I have embraced, and resilience that I have gained. You are a map to my life. Each line of you is the path I've walked, and each spot of you is a moment of growth.

Now, I don't hide you but instead honor you. I nourish you not to erase your presence but to celebrate it. You are a testament to the beauty of living fully, to the grace of aging authentically.

So, dear Aging Skin, I will wear you proudly. You are not a loss but a gift—a reflection of a life well-lived and a heart still full of dreams.

Gratefully,
Me

CHAPTER TWENTY-THREE

Dear Stutter

Dear Stutter

You were my shadow, lingering in every sentence I spoke. You turned simple conversations into daunting challenges, making me question every word before it left my lips. I hated the way you made me pause, stumble, and repeat myself, as if my thoughts were trapped in a maze I couldn't escape.

I would not say much in class, avoid being introduced at social gatherings, and would keep my sentences short in the fear of judgments that mostly came with speaking out. You made me feel small in a world that celebrates eloquence and quick wit. I hated you for silencing me and making me doubt my voice.

But time showed me you weren't the enemy but a teacher who taught me to be patient, with myself as much as with others, the strength to speak, no matter how difficult it was to speak. And it made me a better listener who gives a weight to the words and gives credit to their courage in telling.

Now, I see you differently. You are not a flaw but a unique rhythm in my speech, a reminder that perfection is not a prerequisite for being heard. My voice matters, stumbles and all.

So, dear Stutter, thank you for teaching me resilience and authenticity. You are not a barrier but a bridge to understanding myself and others more deeply.

With newfound confidence,
Me

CHAPTER TWENTY-FOUR

Dear Overthinking

Dear Overthinking,

You are the restless hum in my head, the voice that never stops speaking. Simple choices become debating exercises and silence leads to spiral falls into confusion. You cause me to go back over what is said; examine every piece; and play through every which way until it immobilizes me by "what if".

Sometimes, I feel like you are an enemy who steals my peace and drowns out my clarity. You make me question my instincts, second-guess my choices, and doubt my worth. I have spent so many nights wrestling with you, trying to silence your incessant chatter.

But as much as you exhaust me, you've also taught me valuable lessons. You make me see possibilities others overlook, dig deeper into thoughts others dismiss, and approach problems with care and consideration. You've helped me avoid mistakes and uncover creative solutions.

I've learned that you're not here to hurt me—you're here to protect me, even if your methods are flawed. So instead of fighting you, I'm learning to work with you. I'm setting boundaries, finding balance, and reminding myself that not every thought deserves attention.

So, dear Overthinking, thanks for challenging me to grow. You are not a flaw, but part of my complexity—a reminder that even the loudest storms can be calmed with patience and self-compassion.

With cautious appreciation,
Me

CHAPTER TWENTY-FIVE

Finding Beauty in My Flaws and Strengths

We grow up in a society where perfection is worshiped. Social media is plastered with PR images and filtered lives: energy, accomplishment, and happiness. It's almost as if there is no place for error or mistakes. But through my experience of life, I have learned that real connection, real humanity, finds itself not in what we get right but in what we stumble through. My flaws, like my strengths, have shaped who I am, and they carry lessons I could not have learned any other way.

I kept my flaws locked up in the dark closet for as long as I could remember. My spelling was bad-awful-for such a simple, nearly inconsequential thing, it shamed me. Words have been my way to express love and understanding, and yet those little red squiggly lines on the screen felt to me like some small failures against their worth. But then I realized something in me shifted around. I might not be particularly good at spelling, but God has given me a gift, speaking to peoples' hearts. When someone is feeling broken, I can find the words to lift them, to make them feel less alone. Those moments have taught me that sincerity far outweighs perfection. The power of my words lies not in their flawlessness but in the truth and compassion they carry.

Well, honestly, I cannot count how many times I had procrastinated and stared at seemingly insurmountable tasks as the clock raced against me and pushed them by. But sometimes, in frantic last minutes before the deadline loomed, this is when my creativity and sharp focus have arisen from nowhere - unexpected, yet proven to be essential. Procrastination taught pressure, yes; but it showed me resilience more than anything, that even while I faltered, I managed to recover in time, produce, and get better.

Overthinking has been both a curse and a revelation. My mind often feels like a whirlwind of possibilities running through scenarios until exhaustion takes over. It's paralyzing at times, making me question every decision and every path. Yet, this same overthinking has made me a thoughtful person, one who carefully considers the feelings of others. It has taught me to pause, reflect, and ensure that actions are in keeping with values. Overthinking, though flawed, has been a guide to living more intentionally.

I have always battled with self-doubt, that persistent whisper questioning whether I am enough. It has kept me from seizing opportunities, made me hesitant to celebrate my achievements, and left me second-guessing my worth. But this self-doubt has also driven me to grow. This has stretched me to work harder, learn more, and present even if I feel unworthy. It's taught me the value of perseverance and the beauty of humility. In those moments when I overwhelmed doubt and succeeded, I found within myself a strength that seemed unbreakable.

Then there's impatience—the restless desire I have to make things happen now. It's led to frustration, pushing too hard, too fast. Yet impatience is also a testament to passion. It makes me chase after my dreams with urgency, push for everything that matters to me, and chase after things that I care for with everything I have in me. It reminds me of how much I am invested in my life, in my goals, and in the people that I love.

Failure. The very word feels heavy. I can't count the number of times I have failed, but with each failure, a blow was left that seemed to never heal. However, failure has been my best teacher. It humbles me, reminding me that I am not God, and it reminds me that falling is not crashing. I have fallen every time I have failed, but rose equally every time. I have learned to adapt, grow, and keep going. Failure has taught me resilience, and for that, I am grateful.

What I have come to understand is that my flaws are not burdens to carry or scars to hide. They are threads woven into the fabric of who I am, just as essential as my strengths. My flaws make me relatable, approachable, and real. They remind me of what really bonds us, though: it isn't perfection that connects us. It is only in the crack that light comes in; the struggles give it root; only in our vulnerabilities can true intimacy arise.

So, yes, I'm really bad at spelling. I procrastinate. I overthink. I'm impatient. I have failed far more times than I can recall. But so am I that person who can make people feel seen and valued. I'm that person who finds beauty in connection, someone who thrives under pressure, who feels deep and loves fiercely. My flaws and strengths aren't opposites; they dance together, weaving a story that is uniquely mine.

And that story? It's messy and beautiful, imperfect and whole. It's a story worth celebrating, not despite my flaws but because of them. For they are not just parts of me; they are the heart of me. And in embracing them, I've found not just self-acceptance but a deeper connection to the world around me.

Take a moment, right now, to celebrate your own flaws alongside your strengths. Think about the parts of yourself you've hidden or wished away and ask what they've taught you. Remember the times when your imperfections helped you grow or allowed you to connect with someone else. Honor the whole of who you are, for it is in the messiness, the duality, and the vulnerability that your beauty truly lies. You, just as you are, are enough.

CHAPTER TWENTY-SIX

Imperfect Fairy tales: Love the Flaws of a Perfect World

Perfection is an illusion; the true beauty lies in the moments we've lived through, the cracks we've weathered, and the pieces we've gathered.

Perfection—so desperately sought, so ardently coveted—is but a mirage. True beauty that touches the heart lies not in flawless exteriors but in cracks we have weathered, in wounds we have healed, and pieces of ourselves that we have picked up along the way. Within our hearts we all know it, even though it is sometimes hard to hold onto. The real magic of life doesn't come from perfection; it comes from the imperfections that shape us, make us whole, and remind us that we are human.

Once upon a time, the fairy tale heroes were chiseled from marble, smooth and unblemished, impossible to break. The heroines were lithe, flawless beauties with sparkly happy ends that fell in place effortlessly. But what if the magic doesn't reside in an infinite search for flawlessness? What if it is instead the lopsided smile, the rugged palms, and unruly locks that make them so lovable, so believable, and so real?

Imperfect Fairytales is an invitation to reimagine stories we have known for so long—those timeless classics that have been passed down from generation to generation. It goes against the assumption that heroes and heroines should be molded in some gilded ideal. It celebrates what makes us different-the quirks, the flaws, the imperfections that we hide but which, when embraced, become our greatest strengths.

These are stories not of fixing what's broken but of cherishing what makes us whole. Learning to see the beauty in the cracks and the scars. Discovering that it doesn't need to fit those shiny molds to be loved, successful, or happy. Here's the truth-it's the imperfections that make us who we are. They are the silent storytellers of our lives—the quiet details that carry the weight of our experiences: resilience, humor, love, and growth.

Take Cinderella, for example. In this retelling, she is not just a girl waiting for her life to change. A calloused-handed Cinderella does not hide the strength she has built through years of hardship. Her hands, rough and weathered, tell a tale of endurance. They talk of long nights spent working, of battles fought silently, and of a heart that refused to break no matter how hard life became. These hands, scarred by toil, are a testament to her courage, and they make her more powerful, more inspiring than any delicate glass slipper ever could. She doesn't wait for someone to rescue her; she's already been her own savior.

Then there's Snow White. In the fairytale we know, her beauty is idolized, but in this, Snow White's crooked smile isn't something that needs to be corrected; it is instead the token of her true self. That one small weakness—a smile that does not fit the perfected stylings of her peers—makes her well and truly magical. Her smile is just a testament that there's really joy found on the imperfection of life - that beauty actually lies in some sort of abnormality and may not necessarily bring symmetry, because it is by these quirks, scars, and unpolished parts that human beings give that depth, that warmth, or that reality.

What then was Beauty and the Beast? It isn't about any transformation from a beast to the prince, but rather about an all-transcending love that overcomes the needs for transformation; it is an exact love with scars, with flaws, the way they are. The beast does not have to change into anything but himself to love. And the same goes with Beauty. So their love is not a thing of external transformations but of inward acceptance. They learn to love each other for the beauty within—what makes them imperfectly perfect. Through this love, they both grow, not by becoming what they're not, but by fully embracing the truth of who they are.

These stories—Imperfect Fairytales—are not just for children. They are for anyone who has ever looked in the mirror and wished they were different. They are for those who were told they were not enough, had to change, fit in, be loved, succeed. These tales remind us softly yet firmly that we do not have to be perfect to be worthy. We do not have to hide our imperfections; we must learn to love them. Because in a world obsessed with ideals, the greatest magic we can create is the courage to love ourselves, as we are.

They are not fixing anything. They tell us to be able to find the beauty within our cracks, quirks, and flaws, because these very things speak of resilience, of connection, and of quiet courage to be, at last, really and authentically ourselves. They remind us that imperfection is where it's at—that is to say, where humanity lies.

In a world which has been given to believe the highest goal is perfection, Imperfect Fairytales ventures to tell the world that magic lies in taking the parts within us that were taught to hide from the world: the crooked smile, calloused hands, messy hair–all markers of a life as lived, battle fought, joy shared, love that does not ask us for change. In these stories, beauty is not about being flawless; it is about being whole. And to be whole is to be real.

For when we let go of the pursuit of perfection, we make space for something far more precious: the freedom to love ourselves, flaws and all. And that, truly, is the most beautiful fairytale of all.

CHAPTER TWENTY-SEVEN

The Sweetness of Embracing Flaws

I will show you there are quiet beauties in these tales—a gentleness of not rushing at perfection but really taking the time to find it with imperfection and all. Inviting us softly to look again at ourselves—to see that these are not exactly our perfect times, but truly our messy moments, flawed to be human in every way, that make all the difference and give us that worth.

Imagine the tender satisfaction of a small girl running her fingers through her thick, wild locks as she discovers the story about Rapunzel and her lengthy, unruly, full of life, defying hair: that is precisely what she's carrying around. She feels it, for the first time ever, understood. She doesn't have to fix herself to fit into some mold; she sees in Rapunzel's story that beauty can be found in the very thing she's always thought was a flaw. Or picture the quiet triumph of someone who has carried the weight of scars on their skin—physical or emotional—finding solace in the Beast's journey. In his monstrous exterior, they see a mirror of their own struggles, their own battles fought in silence. They realize they are not alone. The Beast, too, once believed that his scars made him unworthy of love, but it was through accepting his imperfections that he found the truest form of love: the kind that comes from self-acceptance.

These fairytales don't rush to fix what's broken. They do not push for a hasty change or a neat conclusion. They dwell on the cracks—the parts through which the light can pour. They give room for imperfections to speak out and tell stories of growth, strength, and learning. They prove to us that cracks in life are not marks of weakness, but of strength. Each flaw, every scar, serves as a testament of how far we have come-to the battles and wars we won and survived over. These scars do not undermine us; it is what makes our beauty deeper.

CHAPTER TWENTY-EIGHT

Perfection Is Only a Story.

Our imperfections are the footprint of our lives. They're the stories and marks on the skin and souls, marking us for the various moments that change us, or teach us otherwise. The slightly curved-to-the-side crooked smile hides a story of a child laughing through the falling tears, who learned to find happiness even in the hardest moments. Messy handwriting says that this person wrote his or her own story, not perfectly but with conviction. The offbeat laugh, that one that takes you by surprise, that one you try to suppress but fail to do so—this is the laugh of someone who is embracing their quirkiness and refusing to mold into what society expects. The little imperfections, when not hidden, turn out to be our most beautiful features.

These are what make us us, and the more we share them, the deeper the connection. Because someone, somewhere, will see your flaw and know it as themselves. And then you won't feel so lonely anymore.

CHAPTER TWENTY-NINE

Flaws Build Connection

Isn't it interesting? How often we think flaws will repel people from us, when it is, in fact, exactly what attracts people to us. People don't fall in love with perfection. They fall in love with who we are—flaws and all. The authenticity that comes with showing up, not as a polished version of ourselves, but as the raw, unfiltered person who has lived, loved, fallen, and risen again. When we stop hiding behind a facade, when we allow ourselves to be seen in all our messy, beautiful, imperfect glory, we make space for others to do the same. And it is in this space, in this space that accepts and gives way to flaw, that one truly connects.This is the awkward dance move; these are the messy handwriting skills we try so desperately to tuck away into a corner during class. The crooked smiles. These things are what others remember about you. These things stick with people long after conversation ends. These things remind them of themselves-themselves-their own flawed, imperfect, yet beautiful selves. They are the imperfections that bind us stronger than perfection ever could. It is the imperfections we share that allow us to see humanity in one another. And in doing so, we find that we are all the same—imperfect, yes, but perfectly us.

CHAPTER THIRTY

Authenticity is Strength

There is a quiet power in being unapologetically yourself. In standing before the world and saying, "This is me.". I am not perfect, but I am enough." So often, we hide parts of ourselves, thinking they're not worthy of being seen. We put on masks to fit in, to be accepted, to be loved. But what if the love we are seeking already exists within us, just waiting to be discovered when we dare to be authentic?The stories of these imperfect heroes teach us that strength lies in embracing who we are, flaws and all. It's not the flawless princesses or the perfect heroes who change the world but those who stumble and fall and get back up and keep moving forward. They don't look for perfection because they know that the beauty of life is not in its flawlessness, but rather in its mess. They know it well that to be human is to be a work in progress, to be a mosaic of moments: joyful and painful, graceful and messy. In this understanding lies their power.

CHAPTER THIRTY-ONE

A Tale for Every Heart

These aren't merely tales for the 'perfect' princesses and faultless heroes. These are tales for those who dare to dream of a world that doesn't fit them into the ideal mode; these are tales for fighters-the victims of falls, but still get up from the scrapes. They are for those who have gazed in the mirror, wondering whether they were good enough. For the ones who have tried to hide their scars, their quirks, and flaws, for thinking that they weren't lovable.They remind us of how the very things we try to hide in ourselves—the flaws and quirks we try so desperately to erase—are what makes us special. In short, these stories of imperfect heroes resonate with some deep place within all of us. They point out that we are not any less defined or diminished by flaws; we define ourselves through imperfections. And they are just the pieces in the puzzle, which make who we are worthy of love and connection and of acceptance.Because at the end of the day, it's not about being perfect. It's about being real. And in that realness, we find our greatest strength and our deepest beauty.

CHAPTER THIRTY-TWO

Cinderella: The Calloused-Handed Princess

Cinderella had lived her whole life being told that beauty came in soft hands, delicate skin, and gentle grace. Her stepmother and stepsisters constantly reminded her that to be worthy of love or admiration, one had to embody perfection—the perfect appearance, the perfect poise. And yet, Cinderella's hands, weathered by years of hard labor, told a different story altogether. Her hands, now, were quite rough. Their care had paid the price for long days of scrubbing the floors, washing, firing, and living under the harsh rule of her stepmother. Their were calloused, worn, and strength-witnessing testaments of silent resilience and quiet endurance. Every crack of her skin, every rough edge of such hands spoke of such quiet strength needed to survive.

Despite the taunting of her stepsisters, who would mock the calluses and cruelly joke about her "working hands," Cinderella saw something in them that was simply beautiful. There was quiet pride in the way her hands had carried her through years of adversity and a strange comfort in knowing they were a reflection of who she truly was. As she toiled in the kitchen, where candlelight was meager, Cinderella would glance down at her hands, silently thankful for the strength they had provided her. Not just hands-they were representations of survival, dreams held tight amidst the weight of the world crashing down on her.

The news of the royal ball arrived; it was just a distant dream, something that Cinderella would never dare to imagine. A life of ball gowns, sparkling slippers, and the kind of elegance her stepsisters seemed to take for granted was far out of her reach. But all of that changed when the fairy godmother came. The magic transformed Cinderella from a poor servant into a vision of elegance and beauty. She was clad in a shimmering gown, hair perfectly arranged, and glass slippers—the epitome of elegance—placed upon her feet. But as the transformation neared its end, something inside Cinderella hesitated. The delicate hands she now had felt foreign to her. They were smooth, unmarked, as though they hadn't lived, hadn't fought, hadn't endured.The fairy godmother, seeing the look in Cinderella's eyes, moved to change her hands to match the rest of her new look, but Cinderella stopped her. "Why hide what made me, me?" she asked, her voice soft but resolute. "These hands carried me through every hardship. They held my dreams, no matter how small they seemed. They are mine, and they are enough."

For the first time, Cinderella was making the fairy godmother see the depth of her words. She paused, gesturing for a moment and then, in gentle nod, agreed with it. Cinderella's hands remained the same- rough, calloused, and full of stories. She went to the ball, but not as every picture-perfect princess expected her to be. She went as the perfect Cinderella, raw, real, and starkly powerful in her authenticity.

As she danced at the ball, the music swirling about her, Cinderella felt an odd sense of comfort, as if she'd finally found her place not by pretending to be who she wasn't but by embracing everything of herself. She didn't hide behind the roughness of life that had shaped her or rub off the impostor syndrome trying to be what or who someone else wanted her to be. But she stood tall, calloused hands at her sides, each groove on the palms telling the story of her journey.

The prince was enchanted by the mix of awe and admiration on his face while he watched her; it wasn't her unblemished features but the undeniable strength emanating from her presence. "These hands," he whispered softly, not breaking his gaze as they swayed to the dance, "they tell a tale. You have lived, and with it you've gained something that most never will—strength."

At his words, Cinderella's heart swelled. A smile tugged at the corners of her lips. "I have lived every day with these hands," she replied, her voice steady with pride. "I have made a life for myself with them."

The prince, seeing not just her beauty, but the fire in her spirit, was deeply moved. It was in that very moment that he came to realize Cinderella was no damsel in distress, no fragile princess waiting for someone to save. She was a woman who had rescued herself. And that was the most irresistible thing of all. He didn't love her because she was broken; he loved her because she loved every part of herself, from the past to the strength, and from the defects.

When the prince eventually proposed, it wasn't out of a desire to rescue Cinderella from a life of hardship. No, he wanted to stand beside her, to face the future together, to build something lasting—a partnership based on mutual respect, love, and the shared belief that hard work, perseverance, and authenticity were the true foundations of happiness.

Together, they managed to build a kingdom where people could rise through the ranks, not by the softness of hands or the gentleness of their skin, but by the toughness of their souls and the depth of their hearts. They opened schools and training institutes, giving tools to the working class of the kingdom to achieve what they wanted in life. Cinderella and the prince built a society where every person's story was valued, where hard work was not something to be ashamed of but something to be celebrated.

Their kingdom may not have been perfect, but it bloomed with hope, because each individual was recognized for the unique journey they had walked. They no longer hid their scars or tried to cover up the parts of themselves they thought were "flaws." Instead, they learned to wear their imperfections proudly, knowing they were what made them beautiful, what made them strong, what made them human.

Cinderella, with her calloused hands and unassuming strength, was no longer a fairytale waiting to be rewritten. She was the author of her own story, one of resilience, love, and the courage to be exactly who she is. And she proved it in a world that kept telling her that it wasn't good enough, that the best magic was not perfection but the acceptance of ourselves as beautifully flawed.

CHAPTER THIRTY-THREE

Snow White: The Princess of the Unproportionate Smile

Snow White's smile had always been something that had made her feel different, though not in the manner she would have liked. It was not perfectly symmetrical, something that had been pointed out to her time and again, both by her stepmother, the Evil Queen, and by society itself. The left corner of her mouth was curved upward more than the right; it was a small flaw the Queen seemed to obsess over. She would stand before her mirror, gazing at her own reflection, and tell Snow White that beauty was only achieved through balance, symmetry, and grace—things Snow White felt she lacked.She, the Queen with her obsession for perfection, kept nagging Snow White for her uneven smile, stating it made her less beautiful, less deserving of attention. Snow White tried to conceal it, pushing her lips together in a thin line whenever someone gazed at her. But however much she tried, that smile was there-always just a little crooked, just a little uneven. And the more the Queen ridiculed her, the more Snow White became an alien to her own self.

When finally Snow White was running into the forest to evade the Queen, she thought it was running from the mirror and that was her failure. But along with the seven dwarfs she found something, which she wasn't expecting – acceptance. The dwarfs loved her for who she was, not for how she looked, but for the kindness she brought, her laughter, and the warmth of her heart. Snow White didn't need to hide her smile when she was with them. She could laugh with them over their meals, cook with them, and hear their stories around the fire. They didn't care about her smile. They loved her for her spirit.One evening, as they sat together by the warmth of the fire, Snow White found herself feeling vulnerable. She turned to Grumpy, who had always seemed so guarded, so stern, and confessed her feelings. "I hate my smile," she said quietly. "It's crooked, and I feel like it's all anyone ever notices about me. I just wish it were perfect."

This, coming from someone whose rough appearance had always presented him as impossible to get along with, threw her off guard. His voice had softened, and he looked at her with a type of understanding that she hadn't expected. "You think people love perfection?" he asked gruffly. "It's your crooked smile that makes you real. It's part of who you are, Snow White. It's what makes you. you."His words sank deep into her heart. Slowly, Snow White began to understand that her smile was not a weakness; it was part of her, the reflection of her journey, of challenges she had gone through and of the person she had become. Her crooked smile was nothing to hide, but to own. This was a mark of resilience, the love she had for herself even when the world had tried to make her believe she wasn't enough.

And when the prince arrived to wake her from the curse, she didn't need him to kiss her to feel whole. Snow White had learned, deep in her heart, that she was already alive—not because of any outward appearance, but because she had finally learned to be herself. The prince didn't see her crooked smile as something that needed fixing. He didn't see it as a flaw. What he saw was her strength—her strength to be authentic in a world that told her to be anything but.

They sat together for hours, sharing their stories, their dreams, and their hopes for the future. It wasn't the kiss that woke Snow White from her slumber—it was the connection they shared, a connection built on respect, trust, and understanding. He was drawn, not to the beauty of Snow White, but to her spirit: the manner in which she learned to be strong in weakness and beautiful in breakage.Her smile was once something she wore a mask of. As Snow White became the queen, however, it shone for the entire world to witness the beauty, now found in a different form—something she triumphed over. Her twisted smile was present in every portrait, in every painting, a reminder to the kingdom that beauty was not about symmetry, or about fitting into some predefined mold. Beauty was about being real. It was about showing the world your true self, flaws and all, and saying, "This is me, and I am enough."

Her smile was imperfect; however, it became a beacon of hope to everyone who had been told they were never good enough. That symbol reminded them that it is their imperfections that made them who they are-that the things they sometimes hide about themselves are the same things that make them strong, human, and deep.

And so, as Snow White ruled with kindness and wisdom, her kingdom bloomed. A kingdom where imperfection was celebrated, where diversity was embraced, and where everyone, no matter what flaws they might have, was valued. For Snow White had learned, and she had taught her people, that true beauty comes not from perfection, but from the courage to be yourself, to stand proud in your imperfections, and to love yourself, exactly as you are.

And thus, Snow White's smile with all its glorious asymmetry continued to live—not only as an icon of her own story, but as an inspiration for every soul who had ever felt he or she wasn't good enough. In a world where most people seem to be after a perfect body or even a perfect person, Snow White's tale serves as a reminder that it is our imperfections that complete us. And in accepting those imperfections, we find a beauty that no mirror can possibly define.

CHAPTER THIRTY-FOUR

Beauty and the Beast: A Love That Lasts

The outside transformation was from the once-proud prince who had been changed into the Beast, but his heart had changed more profoundly. He was a prince who had once been a slave to his vanity and pride, insensitive to the suffering of others, living for his selfish desires. In this case, all its cruelty was not in removing him from outward beauty that he was so accustomed to but forced him to deal with the ugly features of his own soul. Isolated within his castle away from human sight, it is where he begins to find meaning in terms of humility, compassion, and above all, connection.

Belle was first introduced to him when she did not see the beastly form that people were so scared of. For her, the monster was a mere shell of his pain and struggles. She wasn't repelled by the growls and claws, nor by the fearsome image he presented. Instead, Belle looked deeper, into the part of him that had been buried under years of bitterness and regret. She saw the man he had once been, the vulnerability in his eyes that hinted at the goodness still trapped within, and the longing for love and redemption that he couldn't hide, no matter how hard he tried.

As they spent more time together, their connection grew. What began as an uneasy friendship blossomed into something neither of them could have expected—a bond that transcended appearance and circumstance. It was during their late-night conversations, sharing stories of their pasts and their dreams for the future, that Belle began to understand just how much the Beast had suffered, and how much he had learned. She saw him as not just a cursed creature, but as a man who was given the painful opportunity to grow, to evolve, to find the strength to love again even after he was broken.

One evening, as they sat sitting by the fire side, the Beast's voice broke the silence, heavy with the weight of his doubts. "You've seen me as I am, Belle," he said softly, his eyes downcast. "You have been kind to me, but what if. what if you're only staying because you pity me? What if you loved me because of what I look like and not because of who I am?"

Belle turned to him, her gaze unwavering. She saw the fear within his eyes and the deep insecurity, which still lived on despite all they had experienced together. She lay her hand down softly over his; she could feel the warmth of his skin, the reality of him, not a monster, but a person: a man, hurt and healed just as she had been. "I love you," she said, her voice soft yet resolute, "not for how you look, but for who you are. Your heart, your soul, they are more beautiful than any surface could ever be."

For the first time in his life, the Beast felt a sense of relief wash over him. He had never known love like this—love that didn't come with conditions or expectations, love that saw him as more than a cursed creature. Belle loved him for his heart, for the person he had become through years of pain and growth. And in that moment, he realized that perhaps the curse hadn't just taken away his prince's form but had allowed him to become the man he was always meant to be.

As time went on, the villagers began to grow restless. Their fear and biases fed the flames of their animosity towards the Beast, so they called on him to once again assume human form, resume the appearance of the prince he was only suited to win over the love he felt for them. But Belle, who had developed a sense of protectiveness about the man, refused to be intimidated. And then, when they come to her and demand she do something for them and make the Beast change, she looks at them straight and tells them, "You think perfection is something that can be seen in a mirror. You judge him by what you see on the outside, but you miss what truly matters. He is more human than all of you who sit in judgment. The truth is, perfection is a lie we tell ourselves to feel superior, to make ourselves believe we are somehow more deserving of love. But he-he is real. He is more human than any of you."

The Beast never became the prince he once was again. And he didn't need to. The love that had developed between him and Belle was not based on looks; it thrived in the acceptance of imperfections. And here, they were able to start a new form of haven, not only for those who had found themselves rejected and looked down upon because of their ways of being but for all others in the same situations. They started inviting the outcasts, the misfits, and the broken-hearted, and, together, built a community of love, without beauty but in kindness, compassion, and understanding.

It became a perfect kingdom because it is no longer obsessed with outward appearances. It looked beyond itself and thrived in a new way, imperfections included, because love is not perfect, especially if it looked a certain way or fit within a mold because people could be free to be themselves. The Beast and Belle worked side by side, not as a king and queen, but as two people who had found something more enduring than any outward beauty: a love that was rooted in acceptance and respect.And though the Beast's appearance never changed, it didn't matter anymore. For Belle had shown him that true beauty lies in the soul, in the heart that dares to love even when the world tells it to hide. Their love, born from the courage to be real, to be vulnerable, and to be accepted, became the heart of their kingdom, a kingdom where people were free to love without fear of judgment, and where they could be celebrated not for their perfection, but for their humanity.

In the end, it was the Beast's imperfections and the love they shared that created a beauty more profound than any magic could conjure.

CHAPTER THIRTY-FIVE

A Day Without Beauty Standards

It would start subtly, like an ordinary day of a beginning—only much softer. The sun would have just started coming up and there it was-casting its usual soft golden glimmer upon everything but somehow carrying within itself, unseeable and subtle- this difference-the most insipid difference for starters but mighty quiet. No loud declarations would echo across the sky. It would be as if the world itself had just exhaled a long-held breath, and in that space of exhale, we would find freedom, as if the world finally allowed itself to let go of something it had been holding too tightly for too long.

This morning, the first thing you would see when you opened your eyes wouldn't be the mental checklist of things you have always thought you needed to fix about yourself. No, this time, it would be different. For the first time in your life, you wouldn't be thinking about how you could be better, thinner, younger, or more symmetrical. Instead, it would be showing you things which you have actually never noticed all along: these things that will really matter-things that all the time haunt the shadows created by judgmental thoughts and nagging self doubt within. You shall see your very flaws, about which you made such a killing by hating them, suddenly shine with unwritten beauty-of a beauty unwritten by external influences but by you itself.

Things would then feel lighter. A quiet comfort would settle within you, and a peace, one you've never known. The mirror no longer would just be an instrument of criticism for you; the mirror would reflect on something more for you—something deeper. The cold, unforgiving surface where you often searched for imperfections would end. Instead, it would show your reflection as if someone who loved you with all their heart stood there and saw you not in the perspective of perfection but in the perspective of acceptance.

A mother brushing her teeth and gazing at the reflection in the mirror would no longer concentrate on the lines etched around her eyes. She would see herself as her child sees her: a woman whose eyes hold years of tenderness, whose smile holds decades of love. Those wrinkles? They wouldn't be seen as signs of aging; they would be celebrated as symbols of wisdom and the years spent giving, nurturing, and loving. At that moment, it would be in the depth of her heart and not in the smoothness of her skin.

A young man would look in the mirror and trace the scars on his face—scars that have been with him since his teenage years, reminders of awkward growth, of battles fought with self-esteem. But today, on this quiet revolution of a day, he would see those scars as not imperfections but stories—stories of resilience, of the love his grandmother always told him to carry proudly. And he would smile at himself—not because of how he looked, but because of how he felt. His face, his story, his imperfections, would finally be enough.

It would quietly, yet significantly, be a day of change-one affecting every lifestyle. It would finally be acceptable to wear the face you have always had. There would be no more need to hide the marks, the lines, or even the quirks that truly define who you are. No more zealous efforts to attain someone else's standard of beauty, which was never yours in the first place. For once, you would be seen as you really are: beautiful, real, and whole.

Work would seem different. Where once there had been judgment according to appearance, now would be replaced with something far more honest: respect, admiration, and attention to what truly matters. You wouldn't see a colleague's hair, her weight, or the clothes she wore judged about. Instead, they would be judged by their kindness, their creativity, their ability to make others feel seen and heard. A woman who had always felt the sting of judgment about her weight would find herself recognized for her generosity, her compassion, her wisdom. He was a man who had constantly felt inadequate because of his thinning hair. Yet, suddenly, he would be valued for the warmth he brought into a room, for the laughter he shared, for the way he made others feel at ease.

Social media would change also. The Photoshopped images, the filters, the sleek, unattainable perfection-it would all fall away. In its stead, people will share real and unfiltered moments of their life. There is no more strain to present as perfect. It is the imperfections of day-to-day lives that people should celebrate—the wearing of pajamas in the wee hours of morning, the bad hair days, and the very human moments that they looked absolutely terrible. Pictures would no longer be about showing the world how perfect you could look, but about showing the world who you truly are. It would be raw, real, and breathtaking in its authenticity.

In fashion, the pressure to conform to trends would fade. People would wear what felt good, not what was expected. A man who had always shunned a bright-colored shirt due to the fear of judgment would finally put it on and walk out of the door with his head held high. A young girl would run down the sidewalk in mismatched socks, not because she was making a statement, but because those socks reminded her of a moment of joy when she was first learning how to tie her shoes. There would be no right or wrong way to dress. There would only be freedom—freedom to wear whatever made your heart feel light.

At breakfast tables, mornings would feel softer. There would be no rush to apply makeup or perfect one's appearance before rushing out the door. Instead, families would sit together, taking the time to genuinely see one another—not just as people who shared the same roof, but as individuals with their own stories, their own struggles, and their own beauty. They will laugh openly, tell stories without an effort to impress, and teach their kids about love for self and acceptance of themselves. A mom will look at her daughter's hair and say, "your curls are like wildflowers, beautiful and free." A dad will kiss his boy on the forehead and tell him, "the gap in your teeth is what makes your smile unforgettable, don't hide it ever.

There would be no appearance-related judgments between the children in schools. He with crooked teeth would stop hiding his smile.The girl with a birthmark would wear it as a badge of honor, no longer hiding it in shame but letting it shine as part of what makes her who she is. The children would grow up knowing that what once was thought to be wrong was in fact the thing that made them unique.

The world would not be perfect by the time the sun set over it that evening. But it would be softer. Kinder. More compassionate. People would look at themselves, and each other, in a new light-free from the impossible standards that had bound them for so long. And in this new world, beauty would no longer be measured by symmetry or conformity, but by authenticity, by the courage to be who you truly are.

And, of course, with days and years gone by, all this one day would be living in the hearts and memories of those who had seen it. All would remember what it felt like, not to be judged, but to look into the mirror and see, not just the outside, but to see something inside of themselves. And they would teach their children to pass it on, to reveal to them that the beauty lies in the imperfections, in the raw, unpolished, unapologetic truth of who we are.

It would be a revolution—quiet, subtle, and yet

unshakable. The world would be different. The world would be better.

It is in the creation of a world which celebrates authenticity because people are of value for what they are not for how they look. And beauty is there to be enjoyed, not achieved-recognized, prized, and distributed in all diversity. If we commit to this vision, we can make it a reality. Parents would teach their children not to focus on outer beauty but the beauty within. They would say, "Your worth is not defined by the shape of your body or the color of your skin. You are enough, just as you are. Love yourself, because you are worthy of love." Such teachings would be passed from generation to generation, making it a culture of self-love, acceptance, and authenticity. A New Era of Compassion and Freedom.By the time the sun sets on this dream day, the world may not be perfect, but it will be kinder, gentler, and more compassionate.People will have learned that true beauty is not something to be pursued, but exists already within each of us in all its glorious imperfections. Beauty is not symmetrical or without flaw.

It is messy, raw, and human. It is the laughter we share, the tears we shed, the love we give and receive. This day is not an impossible dream. It is within our reach. It starts with each of us—by embracing our own imperfections, by choosing love over judgment, by teaching others to do the same.

CHAPTER THIRTY-SIX

Together, we can redefine the beauty of this world.

And when life has stopped in all its hurry, for a brief, shining moment, we realize the truth: that beauty was always there inside us. But it's easy to forget in the world that tells us over and over that we need to look this certain way, act a certain way, or even be a certain way to be worthy. We've been conditioned to believe that there is an external realm of beauty, something to chase, refine, and perfect. That is not the truth. The truth is that beauty is not about conformity to a set of standards; it's about the love we give to ourselves, the kindness we show others, and the authenticity we embrace in every moment of our lives. In this world where such truth has become known, we will never be in the urge to become what others want us to be again; we know we are good enough because our hearts will keep saying so.

It begins with us. Each of us has the freedom of choice over looking at beauty from another perspective. Beauty is not determined by numbers in a weighing scale or a piece of paper covered with smoothened-out skin. It's not something that can be found in a magazine or an advertisement on billboards. It's an aspect that dwells within our imperfections, in those marks we bear, telling the story of who we are. It's the laugh lines that form after years of shared moments with loved ones, the freckles that tell of summer days spent under the sun, the scars that reflect the battles we've fought and won. These are the marks of life, and they make us beautiful.

The dream day we hope for—beauty not being confined to a narrow box of societal expectations—is possible, only if we collectively make it a reality. This begins with every one of us rejecting the belief that we have to change for someone to love or accept us. We are worthy, as we are, right now. We don't have to wait until we shed a few pounds, get rid of a wrinkle, or change the way we look. We are beautiful and lovable in this exact moment, in this very condition.

But enough said for this. It cannot be believed simply by us. We have to spread the message to them, especially to the next generation. The world we want to create is where children grow up knowing that they are loved not because they have met some kind of external standard, but because they are kind, compassionate, authentic, and real. And they will grow up in a world where the differences are not judged but celebrated. A world where being yourself—truly, unapologetically yourself—is the greatest form of beauty.

We must teach our children to see beauty in all its forms: in the quiet strength of a grandmother's hands, in the grace of a person with a disability, in the way a friend's eyes light up when they talk about something they love. We must teach them that beauty is in how we treat each other, in how we listen, in how we help one another, in how we show up for the people who need us. Beauty is in the moments of connection, the gestures of love, and the ability to truly see another person for who they are, without judgment.

And we must do this ourselves. We must make this practice every day, to see ourselves first through love eyes, not judgmental. We mustn't see ourselves as crooked anymore when we look in the mirror; we should see beautiful, complete people. We must forgive ourselves for times we haven't fulfilled, yet embrace the truth that we deserve all the love and kindness in this world just because we exist.

Together, we can create a world in which beauty is determined not by others' standards, but by our love, kind gestures, and the authenticity we have for ourselves as well as with each other, and in that world, we would all be enough. And making this dream day a reality happens through the choices we make today. Every time we decide to be gentle with ourselves, every time we decide to see someone for who they are, every time we decide to love instead of judge, we move one step closer to making that world.

Perhaps this is just a small thing, a whisper in a deafening world. But I tell you, all of us can make a difference. And the truth is that if we all stand up to be counted, then we bring all of the rest of humanity up with us. If we fully embrace our imperfections and our complete love of ourselves, we free everyone else to do the same. And when we together shatter those restrictive definitions of beauty that have held us back for so long, we free each other up to shine.

It's not unattainable; it's just around the corner. It begins with a choice we make. To love ourselves is to start; to love our children to be that way themselves; to tell them that beauty begins within us, with the love, with how we connect and connect ourselves, with the ability to hold one's self in all honesty. It starts here, right now, with us.

We shall create our dream day together. Together, we will create a world where beauty does not look for standards that it has been created by people; rather, we look to it with love, kindness, and the authenticity of the giving and receiving. We will create a world where everyone is enough. That world will come when everyone realizes they are just as perfect. And then it will be the world of real beauty.Our dream world is sitting right there, waiting for us to choose it.

In a world where softness settles, and imperfections are looked upon as being the beauty rather than perfection itself, we go back to the thought of wabi-sabi. Wabi-sabi is the Japanese philosophy about beauty in the imperfection of something, and its transience in the cycles of growth and decay. Wabi-sabi teaches that the beauty that is true can be found only in the crack and creases of life and in the wear and tear that have weathered the object or person or even the moment that has been affected by time and experience and rendered uniquely whole in its imperfection. Just as this dream day world would come to appreciate its imperfect humanity, so wabi-sabi is that which enables one to accept that everything that occurs is but momentary, incomplete, imperfect-and that beauty shines forth the greater for that reality. Nothing, after all, is lovelier than what is real.

CHAPTER THIRTY-SEVEN

WABI-SABI

Wabi-sabi is Japanese aesthetic philosophy that emphasizes a beauty of imperfection or impermanence, highlighting the transience and insubstantiality of things; it celebrates the fleeting. It is a form of Zen Buddhism that acknowledges imperfection as part of life's beauty.The concept often has its representations in terms of visual metaphors of a weathered wooden table, cracked ceramic bowl repaired with gold, or a solitary autumn leaf—all highlighting the beauty of flaws and the passing of time. Wabi-sabi teaches us how to find grace in the imperfect and to accept life the way it is rather than in the pursuit of unattained ideals.

In a world that is obsessed with symmetry and flawlessness, wabi-sabi reminds us that true beauty lies in authenticity. Perfection, as society defines it, is sterile and static—an illusion created by unattainable ideals. But flaws? Flaws tell stories. They show resilience, individuality, and growth.

Wabi-sabi is the perfect marriage of two ideas which are inter-related but very different from one another- wabi and sabi. Both words, as described, carry specific meanings but taken together they lead to the philosophy of deep appreciation in imperfection, impermanence, and simplicity.

1. Wabi (侘び)

Originally, wabi was a feeling of loneliness or desolation, especially that of separation from material wealth or societal comforts. In the course of time, it began to convey the beauty found in simplicity, humility, and appreciation for the unadorned world.

Important Aspects of Wabi

Simplicity and Minimalism: Wabi celebrates the unembellished and the understated. It's the beauty of a single flower in a plain vase or the serenity of an empty room with natural light streaming in.

Authenticity: Wabi values what is genuine and unpretentious. A handmade object with slight imperfections is considered more beautiful than a machine-made one.

Relationship to Nature: Wabi represents the subtle beauty of nature -the curve of a branch, the irregularity of a stone, or the weathered texture of wood. Solitude and Peacefulness: Wabi is also about being content in solitude, embracing moments of quiet reflection, and finding peace in simplicity.

2. Sabi (寂び)

Sabi is rooted in the passage of time, focusing on the beauty of aging, wear, and impermanence. It reflects the quiet dignity of things that have endured the years, carrying with them a sense of history and wisdom.

Main Features of Sabi

This Aging Gracefully: Sabi finds beauty in the marks of time, such as the patina on the bronze statue, the crack in the old ceramic bowl, or the yellow pages of a well-read book. It is about liking the marks of time rather than to erase them.

This is Transience and Impermanence: Sabi accepts the fleeting nature of life and beauty. Only for a short time have the cherry blossoms bloomed beautifully.

Melancholic Beauty: Sabi carries a subtle, bittersweet quality—a recognition of the inevitability of change and decay, and finding beauty in that melancholy.

History and Stories: Objects or places that show wear and age become more beautiful because they hold stories of their existence and survival.

The Harmony of Wabi-Sabi

When combined, wabi and sabi create a holistic philosophy:

Wabi brings the simplicity, humility, and rawness of nature.

Sabi brings in depth in time and embraces impermanence and imperfection.

Together they ask us to go slow down, appreciate the present and find beauty in the inconspicuous and the temporary. A chipped teacup has value as viewed from the wabi-sabi perspective, not despite but because of the chip that it tells a story or reminds us of life's fragility and beauty in it.This philosophy is not about objects or aesthetics; it is a way of living. It teaches us to accept ourselves and others, flaws and all, and find peace and joy in the imperfection and impermanence of life.

CHAPTER THIRTY-EIGHT

Kintsugi

Embrace your cracks; they are where your true beauty shines.

Life becomes a continuous trail of pursuit to be perfect, something to be strived for, something that will complete us once and for all. Flawless skin, perfect body, smooth connections, and success unshaken are some of the things we pursue. But what if I had told you that true beauty lies in the cracks, the chips, moments of vulnerability, and stories you carry? What if the very things we've tried to hide or mend could be the sources of our deepest beauty?

This is where the ancient Japanese art of Kintsugi enters our lives. Kintsugi, meaning "golden joinery," is a profound metaphor for life. It is the art of mending broken pottery with gold, silver, or platinum, emphasizing the cracks rather than disguising them. Kintsugi does not aim to erase damage when a teacup, a vase, or any fragile object breaks. Rather, it glorifies the crack by adorning and making it a part of its history. It is no longer a flaw. The gold that fills the cracks symbolizes both repair and transformation. It takes the broken to something entirely new, something more precious than what it was initially.

Imagine: a delicate teacup, once perfect and smooth, now broken into pieces. In the eyes of the world, maybe this is considered broken, maybe even unworthy of being kept. But in the world of Kintsugi, the teacup is not discarded. Instead, the cracks are carefully filled with shimmering gold, adding to its life anew. The gold does not hide imperfections. No. It makes them, in a way, the very feature that makes the teacup beautiful and irreplaceable. What was once broken becomes, in a sense, more valuable than ever before.

Isn't that such a beautiful reflection of life? Just like that teacup, we all have our cracks—our scars, our heartbreaks, our failures. Life has a way of chipping away at us, leaving marks on our hearts, our minds, our bodies. For the wounds we have is what defines us. But these we should not hide, but reveal because it makes us who we really are. In embracing imperfections, we give ourselves the chance to mend in the deepest sense possible, to be allowed to open our cracks for the filling with golden energy of love, kindness, and acceptance like in Kintsugi, that puts its pottery gold.

Think of the last time you went through a tough time—maybe it was a loss, a painful mistake, or a moment of deep vulnerability. In those times, it can feel like we're losing pieces of ourselves, like we're becoming less than who we were before. But in reality, we're not losing ourselves. We are evolving, transforming, becoming more. We are writing our own golden lines on the fabric of our being, lines that speak of resilience, growth, and love.

We have our cracks just like the teacup. And our cracks are not something to hide. They are our gold, our living history, the evidence of all we have overcome. Those cracks can be mended with the love we give ourselves and the support we receive from others. And whenever we heal, whenever we fill our cracks with gold, then we shine in ways that we would never even imagine ourselves to be before. The broken parts of ourselves are sacred, a reflection of the journey we have taken, and a symbol of the beauty that springs from pain.

Kintsugi teaches us about not being ashamed of brokenness. The process of mending something fragile with gold is not only about repairing—it is about honoring what has been, what will be, and what is. Every crack and every scar has a purpose. Every tear shed, every bruise, every stumble, adds richness to the life we lead. The things that have hurt us, the parts of ourselves we thought were flawed, are the very things that give us depth and authenticity. They are the gold filling the cracks of our hearts.

The teacup, after being repaired by Kintsugi, is now more beautiful than it ever was before. It has a story to tell, a depth of experience that a perfect cup could never have. In the same way, we too are made more beautiful by our experiences, by the cracks that life has etched into our souls. We are no longer merely perfect, glossy versions of ourselves. We are real. We are human. And we are glorious in our imperfection.

So the next time you feel broken or not enough because of your flaws, remember the teacup. Remember that the cracks in your life are not something to hide. They are the marks of your survival, your growth, your transformation. And like that teacup, you too can be mended with golden love—love for yourself, love for others, and love for the beautiful, imperfect journey you've lived.

Embrace your cracks. Fill them with gold. And let the world see you for the unique, irreplaceable masterpiece that you are. Because, just like the teacup, your imperfections don't make you less; they make you more. They make you you. And that is the greatest beauty of all.

CHAPTER THIRTY-NINE

The Art of Kintsugi: Repairing the Broken with Gold.

The Japanese art of **kintsugi**, for instance, is one of the most famous expressions of wabi-sabi: a technique used in the repairing of broken pottery with lacquer mixed with gold, silver, or platinum. A broken teacup isn't glued back together and hidden; instead, it's highlighted with precious metals that make the break beautiful and more beautiful than it was before.

This practice encapsulates the heart of wabi-sabi:beauty is imperfection. The gold does not conceal the flaw; it underscores and elevates the teacup to a magnificent rank. It exalts the notion that a thing's beauty lies not in its perfect state but in life signs it had. The sown-together teacup, with golden threads, testifies to survival and transformation.

The process of kintsugi is not merely just fixing something in a concrete, tangible sense but involves the philosophy that is carried forward in life's challenge. The way a piece of ceramics, once teacup, gets some new lease on life upon kintsugi, as does every person upon finding themselves challenged, and such cracks of our lives and struggles will be seen only as elements of strength.

The Beauty of Aging: A Teacup with History

Consider the old teacup that had been passed down generations and generation after generations. Both time and usage had dented it. The brightness of a once brilliant glaze could have worn off on it, and the edges must have softened due to the excess hands that handled it for so many years. That old teacup now bears a story; an inheritance. Wear and tear do not signal the degradation of something but mark the life of something.

In the context of wabi-sabi aging is something that should not be feared and, therefore, hidden but accepted. The teacup, with its faded color and worn edges, speaks to the fact that perfection and youth are not beautiful; rather, beauty is that unique patina created with time. The wrinkles in our faces, the silver in our hair, and the scars we bear-all these are part of the beautiful tapestry of our existence.

A Teacup in the Present Moment: Finding Peace in the Imperfect

Lastly, the teacup symbolizes yet another characteristic of **wabi-sabi:the love of the present**. While in the teacup, we are again brought to the simple things of life-the warmth of the tea, the momentary solitude, or perhaps friends by our side. It may be imperfect, but in so being, the teacup is perfectly proper for its use in the present. It serves us as much as we serve ourselves by embracing the present.

It is in that crack that life finds meaning; perfection, after all, cannot hold it. This teacup reminds us that nothing lasts forever and we're constantly changing like this very cup. Peace is realized through accepting the imperfection, letting us be just who we are, every instant.

A Teacup as a Metaphor for Life

The wabi-sabi teacup teaches that imperfections are not things to be feared or hidden but embraced. Every chip, crack, or stain is part of its history, and it is these imperfections that make the teacup-and by extension, us-truly beautiful. Amidst a world that frequently values perfection, wabi-sabi encourages one to look beyond the surface to appreciate the depth, uniqueness, and authenticity that accompany imperfection.

So, taking your tea from your aged, cracked china mug, remind yourself that it is not those things that are perfect and beautiful but rather those that have been handled by the imperfections in life, just like any of us.

CHAPTER FORTY

Wabi-Sabi to Life

Aging Gracefully:

Aging isn't something to fear; it's an honor. Wrinkles, silver strands, and the softening of once-vibrant features are the marks of a life fully lived. Every wrinkle on the face tells a story of laughter shared with loved ones, quiet moments of contemplation, and battles fought. The silver hair is a crown of wisdom earned from experiences, a testament to resilience, to the tears shed and the joy found. Wabi-sabi teaches us that aging is not a process of decay but an art of grace. Every sign of aging is a line in the story of a well-lived life. Imperfections on our body therefore mark us as a person who has been courageous enough to face passing time head-on while not hiding from it.

Healing and Resilience:

Just like the shining gold seams on a kintsugi bowl, our emotional scars do not mark a blemish of shame but rather the shining lines of healing and strength. They speak of battles we have fought—pain that once threatened to break us, but which, through time, has shaped us into something stronger, something more beautiful. Each scar represents a moment of resilience, of healing that transformed us from fragile to fierce. It's through these cracks that we find our true light. The struggles we face, the grief we carry, and the scars we bear are not signs of our weakness but of our profound capacity to endure, heal, and rise. These imperfections add to our character, making us more human, more compassionate, more whole.

Nature's Flaws:

In the natural world, imperfections are celebrated. A gnarled tree, twisted by the winds, stands as a symbol of endurance. The jagged coastline, the storms that have molded it for centuries, is a testament to the passage of time. Even bruised fruit is pretty charming; this reminds us that life is not put into straight lines we force upon it. For wabi-sabi, such imperfections are not just accepted but cherished, proof that life is not to be confined in some perfect mould. And, just like that nature develops by her very imperfect manner; we grow like this as well. We only are because we have all that makes us unperfect; therefore, to cherish our flaws as something precious only means being the world.

Practicing Wabi-Sabi In Love or Relationship

In a sense, wabi-sabi calls people to transcend such idealism from seeing their would-be "ideal" love companion as complete and ideal;. It's not perfection; it is those quirky, vulnerable things that are the real stuff we share. Unplanned moments, awkward silences, spilled coffee laughs, and understanding moments in our weaknesses are the real things that bond us. And our relationship, after all, is not about being flawless, but rather it is supposed to be real. It is in the broken moments, the patches of vulnerability, that love deepens and grows. A connection formed on authenticity will always outshine one based on perfection.

In Creativity

In the world of creation, wabi-sabi reminds us that imperfection is not a fault but a feature. An uneven brushstroke, a slightly crooked vase, or a melody that wavers in its execution—these are not failures, but signs of humanity's touch. These imperfections make the work soulful, making it uniquely ours. A flawless piece of art may be spectacular, but it lacks the depth, the story, that comes from the imperfect human hand. Creativity, like life, prospers in imperfection. And it is through embracing this imperfection that true beauty is born.

Self-Love

Wabi-sabi invites us to give up the pursuit of unattainable perfection and to embrace the things that make us unique. The lines on our faces, the imperfections in our bodies, the stories of our lives etched into our skin—these are not flaws, but parts of our essence. Every imperfection, every quirk, is a building block in the person we've become. To love ourselves is to honor our flaws, to see them as the beautiful, irreplaceable marks of our journey. In the same way we love a cracked mug or a bent tree, we should learn to love ourselves as we are because it is where our

imperfections make us strange.
Flaws Are Perfection

Flaws are no failures; they are evidence of a life lived with authenticity and grace. They are proof that we have stumbled, fallen, and risen. They are the times when we are tested, yet we manage to continue on because of the cracks. A bowl, when cracked and mended, is even more beautiful, more unique. These imperfections in us are what make us even more beautiful with the laughter and pain we lived, with love and growth. It is not a blemish to be ashamed of but rather something to be cherished.

In a world obsessed with perfection as the ultimate goal in all, it is wabi-sabi, reminding us all that the good, the not-so-perfect, the never-finished are beautiful in every way. A flecked complexion, a break in the heart, a cup chipped—all treasuries for unique pieces to a greater beauty. Perfection may be antiseptic and sterile, while imperfection thrives on interpretation and meaning. It is from our weaknesses that we learn how to be kind, how to be compassionate, and how to grow. We were not born perfect; we are meant to be real.

To live with wabi-sabi is to live with elegance, accepting that our flaws are not barriers to beauty but beauty itself. Every crack, every wrinkle, every scar speaks of the life we have lived and the beauty within us. Let us, then, embrace our imperfections for they are what make us whole. And so, in embracing these imperfections, we will find the truest beauty of all.

Natural Wisdoms: Wabi-Sabi of Nature

Nature teaches us in a rather incredible way by its imperfections, its transience, and it's beautiful uniqueness. Imagine how trees twist, leaves curl, and creatures proudly wear their flaws-it's as if nature itself whispers a secret: imperfection is not just acceptable; it's worth celebrating.

The Crooked Tree: Symmetry in Imperfection

Have you ever walked through a forest and noticed a crooked tree standing among its perfectly upright counterparts? Most people would walk by and dismiss the tree as "flawed." But what they have here is a crooked tree that, despite its imperfections, is standing strong.

Imagine the scene when a storm rolls in. Tall, erect trees snap under the forceful winds, their trunks not curvable. But the bent tree? It bends and moves with the storm, but still stands unbowed. Flaws in a tree do not make it weaker, but in bending, giving in, this very ability is stronger. In much the same way, twists of life sculpt us. Trials, tribulations, unexpected turns? They break nothing; they strengthen, harden. So, the next time life throws a storm your way, don't fight it—bend with it. You'll come out stronger.

The Uneven Leaf: Diversity is Beauty

Imagine walking through a park and spotting a leaf that

is not symmetrical. One side is smaller, the veins twist in random patterns, and it doesn't look like the others. A child might say it is broken and ask, "Why is this leaf broken?" The response is easy: "It's not broken. It's unique."

Just like that leaf, each of us is one-of-a-kind, shaped by life in our own special way. Our imperfections—our quirks, our differences—are what make us beautifully unique. Think of how many leaves fall from a tree—no two are the same. Just like us, each person carries their own individuality. Imperfection tells a story. It's a reminder that it's okay to be different—it's actually where beauty resides.

The Imperfect Animal: Patterns That Tell Stories

Think of the creatures of nature, each one with its own imperfections. There is a butterfly, so delicate and free, even if it has a torn wing. Or a dog with mismatched eyes, imperfection making it the most adorable thing in the room. A zebra with uneven stripes? Not a mistake, but a living work of art, whose stripes tell a story all their own. These imperfections make animals intriguing, endearing, and full of character. Life's differences don't diminish us; they make us more captivating. What sets us apart is often what makes us stronger, more relatable, and more real.

The Broken Shell: Scars as Stories

Imagine walking along the beach, the waves washing up and down with you. Suddenly, something catches your eye: a broken seashell half-buried in the sand. You might just kick it out of the way, but then you see something magical. The cracks? They reveal intricate, hidden patterns—patterns that would've been invisible if the shell hadn't been broken.

Just like the seashell, our scars, whether emotional or physical, do not indicate damage but growth. Every crack in the shell is a piece of its journey, every scar a testament to survival. What's broken doesn't have to be discarded; it can be more beautiful, more precious, because it's been through something. So when you look at your own scars, remember: They're not flaws-they're your stories, written in the language of life.

The River Stone: Smoothed Through Time

Consider a river stone. Freshly flung into the water, it's a jagged rock, full of sharp edges and points. However, with the passage of time, the river smooths out the stone. The edges lose their rough feel, and the stone is polished-not because of brute force, but patience. It's the constant gentle flow of water that transforms the stone into something more smooth, more beautiful.

As the stone to that river, we get polished by life. Each surge of hard time is a bit of a sculptor to us, smoothening us out and shaping us. Trust the process because you are in growth, development, and beauty with time, much like the stone. The scrapes and bruises? These're just part of the flow.

How to Apply Nature's Wisdom to Life?

It has crooked paths. Life's not a straight line. Like that crooked tree, embrace all your bends and twists. That is what made you stronger and more adaptable to life. Thus, when the road bends to turn you off the course, it is where you find your strength.

See Beauty in the Small Details: Life isn't perfect, and that's okay. The small quirks—the way a leaf's veins twist or a shell's crack—are where the real beauty is. Find beauty in your imperfections. They're what make you uniquely you.

Honor the Stories in Scars: Your scars—whether physical or emotional—are part of your story. They're proof of your survival. Like a broken shell, your marks aren't flaws; they're the chapters that tell of everything you've overcome. Celebrate them.

Celebrate Individuality: Just as the animals do with their odd eyes or irregular stripes, differences are what truly connect us to the world at its most intimate levels. Learn to love your weirdness. It's your superpower.

Trust the Process: The river smooths a stone over time. Just like that, life is honing you in. Trust in the journey — the highs and lows, messy in-betweens: it's how you are refined into something much more beautiful than you can dream of. Exactly where you're meant to be.

Nature's blemishes are actually its greatest boon. From twisted trees to jagged stones, it teaches us to embrace imperfections rather than rectify or cover them up. So let us take a lesson from nature and, instead of disguising our faults, learn to trust the process and find beauty in the unexpectedness of it all. The cracks, the chips, and the bends do not break us; they make us who we are. And that, my friend, is a masterpiece.

CHAPTER FORTY-ONE

The Heart of Imperfection

As we approach the final pages of this journey, we come to understand something profound: Imperfection isn't just a part of life—it is life. Every crack in a heart, every rough edge of a soul, every asymmetrical moment is not a blemish, but a part of our unique, tender beauty. This book has been a love letter to those imperfections, reminding us that the things we once considered flaws are actually the most precious parts of who we are. There's a twisted tree that bends with the wind, a pot mended with gold cracks, and a child's messy, unpolished smile—these aren't just objects, they are stories. Stories of resilience, of growth, of strength. They whisper to us that it is the broken, the bent, the imperfect that carry the deepest beauty, the most genuine warmth.

In a world that says we have to be flawless to be loved, we forget our most beautiful moments are the ones when we step away from perfection and become honest, vulnerable beings. The world doesn't need another perfect face or flawless life. It needs the real, the messy, the unapologetically human. It needs your light, your scars, your crooked smile, your well-worn hands.Your imperfections are not your flaws; they are the scars of your journey. Each one is a testament to your strength, your resilience, and the beauty of living authentically in a world that tries to define you. True beauty is not in meeting standards—it's in embracing your unique story, every twist, turn, and mark along the way.

You see, perfection is only an illusion, a fleeting shadow.

But imperfection, now that is the profound and unshakable truth that makes us what we are. Your laughter lines are the lines on the faces of years lived full of joy and joy is imperfect. Your freckles are the tales written on your skin by the sun. The marks on your body, stretchy and curved, narrate tales of growth and of change, of transformation to who you are and mean to be. Every little thing that you once thought was too much or too little—those are the things that make you uniquely, wonderfully, beautifully you. So as you close this book, take a deep breath. Hold it. And then let go of all the pressure to be something you're not. Embrace what's real, embrace what's yours. Because your imperfections are not your weaknesses—they are your power. They are the soft, golden cracks that let your light shine through. Let go of this idea about perfection and hold on tight to the gift of just being wonderfully, unapologetically human-you are enough. Your brokenness doesn't need to be fixed; it is already pretty perfect in its own special way. They are really the key to a real life of authenticity, one of love and joy.

The world does not require perfection from you. The

world requires that you are you. And that, my dear, is a thing of greater beauty than any ideal which may ever be flawless.

Perfection is a myth we were taught to chase, but real beauty lies in the cracks, in the things we think make us incomplete. The scars we hide are the stories that make us whole, the flaws we hide are the parts that make us worthy of love. You are not a finished product to be perfected; you are a masterpiece in progress, and every imperfection is a stroke of your own unique, irreplaceable beauty.

Live in love, live in elegance, and with the fullest embracing of the perfectly imperfect self.

You are enough, just as you are. **You are beautiful, and that is the most beautiful thing of all.**

Let that sink in, deep into your bones: **You are already enough.**